The Awakened Mindset: The Epistemic Ripple Effect

Created by Nina Marie Maldonado

*As ONE **piece of** large ice can create a tsunami and wash out an existence, one tiny pebble can create a ripple that can spread to shores leaving waves of change through the ripples in the sand of time.*

Let's create an Epistemic **RIPPLE** *Effect spreading wisdom, compassion, and peace with the promise of a clearer* ***perception*** *and the promise for a more cherished*

PRESENT MOMENT.

Dedicated to my son, ***Sabah Skye,***

You are the *creator* of your *reality;* make sure you use some color and don't be upset if you color outside the lines. This is your ***Masterpiece.*** Create the life you want and deserve. *Make sure you live your wildest* dreams and **always know that**

***I love you* through and through.**

To my Grandmother,

Thank you for always being my most consistent person growing up and always being there, and for always doing what's right even when others did not agree with it and teaching me integrity, early on.

FOREVER GRATEFUL AND BLESSED!

Save the Children!!!

Disclosure

The author of this book holds no animosity toward any aspects mentioned in this book and anything mentioned in this book is solely for educational purposes.

This is the physical reality of our existence; however, it does not have to be our emotional reality, and that's the choice we should be allowed to make. If you get offended by this book, then that means you are in the right place.

Enjoy Reading,
Learning, and Rewiring.

Remember this,
Pain is inevitable,
Suffering is a choice

You can't control anything,
but how you let it affect you.

How do you choose
to let things
affect
you?

ISBN: 979-8-234-04125-8

Special Thanks

I would like to thank everyone who tried to stand in my way throughout my life. Not only did you not succeed at trying to keep me down, but you motivated me to keep going to become the person I knew I would be. For your limits were only a reflection of yourself and were the very mechanisms that gave me power to succeed so that I could come back and show you that other people's beliefs do not have to dictate your life. I hope you enjoy this book.

To the Real Ones who have been there,
I Appreciate you to the Fullest.

Honorable Mentions

Thank you, *Transformation Academy*, for all the knowledge, lessons, and skills, and a BIG Special Thanks to *Joeel and Natalie Rivera*, I appreciate you both so very much. You both helped create this vision. I will continue to pay it forward.

Thank you to *Sufani at Place of Bliss* for all your knowledge! Namaste! Keep Shining!

Music has been my greatest inspiration throughout my life.

To music, thank you for always being
my biggest comfort and motivator.

To those artists who have kept it real, thank you.

Real eyes, Realize, Real lies

Table of Contents

The Authors Journey to
"The Awakened Mindset: The Epistemic Ripple Effect" 12

Introduction: Writers Eat for Life 18

The Awakened Mindset Mission Statement #1 23

Part 1: The Human Condition 24

Chapter 1: Understanding the System:
Your Mind, Your Programming, Your Reality
1. Knowledge Architecture:
   Your Personal Structure of Knowledge 26
2. Mindset: The Foundation of Your Being 27
3. Belief Systems:
   The Fundamental Convictions
   that Shape Your Mindset 27
4. Perception: The Reality You Construct 28
5. Reality: Physical (Objective)
   & Emotional (Subjective) Reality 28

Chapter 2: Cultivating an Awakened Mindset
1. Epistemology: The Study of Knowledge 29
2. Epistemic Principles:
   Developing Your Epistemic Compass
   Using Principles for True Knowing 30
3. The *Epistemic Ripple* Effect:
   The Epistemic Principles for
   Awakening Your Mindsets 32
4. The Awakened Mindset: The Conscious Awakening 34
5. Subconscious Mind: The Vast, Hidden information 36

Chapter 3: The Prison Program
1. Programmed Mindset: The Subconscious Prison 37
2. The Mental Matrix:
   The Infrastructure of
   Your Subconscious Prison 39
3. Worried Mindset: The Thief in Your Mind 41
4. Guilt Programming: The Internal Accuser 43

5. The Imperfection Trap:
The Programming of Fundamental Flawed 45
6. The Monkey Mindset:
The Restless Engine of Your Prison 47
7. Stolen Focus: The Ultimate Robbery 49

The Awakened Mindset Mission Statement #2 51

Part 2: The Program 52

Chapter 4:
Everything Down to Your Core Comes from Something Before
1. The Insidious Nature of Stolen Focus:
Why Your Attention is the Ultimate Prize 52
2. The Mechanisms of This Grand Theft:
The Initial Trap 53
3. The Consequence:
The Fabrication of Fear, Hate, and Division 54
4. Understanding 4 D's for
Creating Fear, Hate, & Division 55
A. Distract: The First Stage of Disorientation:
Weakening Your Connection 56
B. Disengage: Cultivating Apathy and Isolation 57
C. Disarm: Stripping Away Critical Defenses 58
D. Destroy:
The Fragmentation of Shared Reality 59

Chapter 5: The Power of Programming:
The Unseen Architect: Mental Programming
1. The Fear Factor: The Ultimate Lever of Control 60
2. Hate Cycle: The Weaponization of Division 63
3. Victim Mentality:
The Abdication of Personal Power 66
4. The Algorithm Mind:
The External Architect of Your Prison 69
5. Consumer Culture:
The Endless Cycle of Desirous Programming 72
6. Performance Pressure:
The Relentless Grind of Conditional Worth 75
7. Cultural Programming:
The Invisible Blueprint of Your Reality 78

Chapter 6: The Depths of Cultural Programming: Your Inherited Mind's Construction 81

1. General Belief Systems: The Core of Your Inherited Mind 84
2. Programming Through Subconscious Influences: The Unseen Architects of Your Reality 86
3. Programming Through the Power of Habit: The Automation of Your Reality 87
4. Programming Through Religion: The Habitual Architect of Faith and Morality 89

Chapter 7: Societal Programming: The Labyrinth of Social Engineering and Civic Indoctrination

1. Programming Through Ideologies: The Political and Social Architects of Reality 91
2. Programming Through Language: The Unseen Architect of Your Perception 93
3. Indoctrinated Education System: The Formal Architect of Your Inherited Reality 94
4. Programming Through the Healthcare System: The Authority Over Body and Being 96
5. Programming Through Economic Systems: The Architects of Desire and Worth 98
6. Historical Narratives: The Architects of Collective Memory & Identity 99
7. Programming Through Scientific & Technological Paradigms: The Architects of Accepted Reality 101

Chapter 8: Programming Through Trauma: The Architect of Survival Responses and Fragmented Self 101

1. Generational Curses Programming Through Generational Trauma: The Echoes of Unresolved Pain 103
2. The Silent Generation (1928-1945): Programmed by Scarcity and Sacrifice 105
3. The Boomer Generation (1946-1964): Programmed by Post-War Abundance & Shifting Authority 106

4. Generation X (1965-1980):
Programmed by
Disillusionment and Self-Reliance 108
5. The Millennial Generation (1981-1996):
Programmed by Digital Connectivity
and a World of High Expectations 110
6. Generation Z (1997-2012):
Programmed by Hyper-Connectivity,
Global Crises, and Authentic Imperfection 112
7. Generation Alpha (2010-2025):
Programmed by Immersive
Digital Reality and Inherited Global Crises 114

Chapter 9: Programmed Perspectives:
The Invisible Lenses Shaping Your Reality 117
1. Sticks and Stones Programming: Words Do Hurt 118
2. "If You Have Nothing Nice to Say,
Don't Say Nothing at All":
The Programming of Suppressed Truth 119
3. Programming Through Disney Movies:
The Enchanted Architect of Idealized Reality 121
4. Lining Up, Wait Your Turn, No Cutting":
The Programming of Social Order 123
5. Fire Safety Drills:
Order, Obedience, & Emergency Compliance 124
6. D.A.R.E.'s Unintended Consequences:
Fueling Curiosity, Rebellion,
and Economic Pathways 125

Chapter 10: Programming Through Emotion:
The Affective Feedback Loop
1. Programming through Media:
Media as the Modern Propaganda Machine 127
2. External Validation & Attention Seeking Behavior 129
3. The Addictive Personality:
A Programmed Vulnerability 133
4. Desensitization: The Silent Programmer 136
5. Music as the Program: The Sonic Programmer 139
6. Entertainment: The Alluring Programmer 142

Chapter 11: April Fools: The Architecture of the Joke
1. The Architecture of the Joke:
   The Ritual of the Fool 145
2. The Three Pillars of the Fo
   2.1. The Temporal Fool: The Calendar Hijack 146
   2.2. The Spiritual Fool: The Mandate of Fear 147
   2.3. The Tribal Fool: The Box of Isolation 148

The Awakened Mindset Mission Statement #3 149

Part 3: Breaking Free

Chapter 12: The Journey to the Awakened Mindset 150
1. Quantum Consciousness:
   The Fabric of Reality and Awareness 152
2. Christ Consciousness:
   The Embodied Freedom Beyond Programming 153
3. Quantum Consciousness and Christ Consciousness:
   The Unified Field of Liberation 153
4. Consciousness and Conscience:
   Pillars of the Awakened Mindset 154
5. Consciousness and Deep Focus:
   Cultivating Intentional Presence 155

Chapter 13: The Techniques for Awakening Your Mindset
1. The Arsenal to Liberation:
   Techniques for Combating
   Negative Programming 157
2. Mindfulness Meditation:
   Practices for Reprogramming Your Mindset 159
3. CBT Techniques for Reprogramming:
   Your Simple Guide 161
4. NLP Techniques for Reprogramming:
   Your Simple Guide 166

Part 4: Subconscious Audit:
Plan of Action for Reprogramming

Chapter 14: The Audit of Your Inner World 172
1. The Archive of Experiences:
   The Data Bank: Where Your Past Lives 173

2. The Pattern Recognition & Automation Engine:
The Habit Maker:
Your Autopilot 175
3. The Belief Formation & Reinforcement Systems
The Internal Rulebook:
Your Core Operating Principles 177
4. The Emotional Command Center:
The Feeling Trigger:
Your Instant Reactions 179
5. The Motivation and Drive Source:
The Hidden Driver:
Your Unconscious Urges 181
6. The Protective Mechanism
The Gatekeeper of Change:
Your Inner Resistance 183
7. The Symbolic Communicator:
The Inner Voice:
Your Intuition & Dreams 185

Chapter 15: Overcoming the Programming
Brick by Mindful Brick 187
Overcoming the Programming:
Brick by Mindful Brick:
Methods for *Breaking Free* 187-212
2. Generational Curses:
Identifying Patterns to Break the Habit 213
3. Key Takeaways Across Generations 214

The Awakened Mindset Mission Statement #4 **215**

Chapter 16: It's a Wrap: Welcome to the Awakened Mindset 216
Finale: The Great Schema:
The Conductor of Your Symphony 217

Comprehensive Bibliography 219
Certifications 227
Research and Rewire Literature 228
Socials 235
Final Quote & Farewell 237

Remember,

once you read this book, there is no turning back….

The Authors Journey to "The Awakened Mindset: The Epistemic Ripple Effect"

Nina Marie Maldonado is a self-healed, intrinsically motivated, meticulous, conscientious individual who basically got tired of her own bullshit. Therefore, one day, just deciding that she was no longer going to continue to live in a constant self-created state of suffering and would aim to become the best version of herself. Given years of turmoil, disappointment, pain and suffering, and extreme PTSD, she decided to use the pain to learn and motivate herself into greatness. Nina was trapped in victim mentality, hindered by limited beliefs and toxic mindsets that led her onto the very path that created the trauma that negatively impacted her life during her earlier years. By continuing the generational loop, she found herself in the same situations that she judged so harshly as a child while gaining a broader understanding that life is not about being able to control everything but being able to control the way you let life affect you.

Through various experiences, she was able to form a clear understanding on how the human being operates and has studied for many years on how to change the mind, emotions, and behaviors to ideally heal from the many years of trauma and break free from the programming that kept her limited for years. She has used herself as an experiment to test different methods to rewire the human mind and has been extremely successful in achieving her mission. Not only has she used the knowledge from personal experiences, but she has also taken years of classes, read hundreds of books, and has done immense research to achieve this very goal.

After watching many videos and reading a few Joe Dispenza book's including *Supernatural and Break the Habit of Being Yourself,* did she realize what she needed to do to ultimately change her entire life for the better. The first thing she did was balance her energy. From years of chaos and over stimulation, she was extremely programmed in survival mode. To break free from survival mode was very challenging. Therefore, she felt the best way to do that would be to clear her energy. She began to take energy healing courses and became an Ultimate Natural Healer after successfully completing over 200 hours of energy healing courses ranging from Advanced Reiki to Color and Art Energy Healing to Chakra Healing to Hand Mudras and many more. However, she did not take those classes to become a Reiki Practitioner or Energy Healer for others, it was for herself, so she could clear her own energetic space.

Once her energetic space was clear, she still felt that survival instinct kicking in which then made her realize that the journey must continue. She found herself taking Self-Healing and Self-Care classes which then led into more spiritual practices, Yoga, Spiritual Life Coach, Shamanic Art Therapy and Art Therapy Classes. She took a course on Focus Mastery and Breakthrough and how to change the way you look at things in life, and it really started to open channels in her mind for new areas of thinking and learning.

Although there were still many times when she found herself back into old patterns and ways of thinking, she really yearned to understand the way her mind worked and how to change it. She noticed during a series of Law of Attraction courses that there was something missing from just putting a thought into existence. "You need to feel it" but how do you feel it if you have beliefs that limit you from feeling it? That is when she realized that there was a missing step to this. Then her breakthrough came when she then retook a Mindfulness course, and it changed the way she saw life and her whole experience then elevated.

After completing the Mindfulness course again, she began taking classes on mindset and belief systems and that's when the spark went off in her brain and she realized, "I am programmed wrong". She then took classes on Emotional Intelligence, Rational Emotive Behavior Techniques, Cognitive Behavior Therapy, Neuro-Linguistic Programming, and even Hypnosis which then led her to various pieces of literature, *Mind Programming,* and *Choices and Illusions* by Eldon Taylor, which then led to another informative book called *Dark Psychology and Manipulation* by William Cooper, using, none other than Neuro-Linguistic Programming as a technique for mind control.

Nina was deeply programmed and to truly become her best version, she needed to restructure her beliefs and mindsets and reprogram her own mind. This is why it was so crucial for her to master all aspects of these habitual practices to really understand how they work positively and negatively. She then radically changed everything she consumed on a daily basis and only allowed herself to be exposed to a specific set of beliefs and mindsets. Only uplifting, motivating music and entertainment. No more politics, no more news, no more fake reality, and only limited and controlled fake dopamine. She needed to see the change in the way she felt when she consumed less of physical reality to allow her subconscious to understand that many of her worries and guilts came from outside of her and were deeply influenced by physical reality.

In addition, she continued reading more books and doing immense research on these topics and continued with taking classes to rewire her mindsets and beliefs including Confidence Coach, Happiness Coach, Empowerment Coach, Forgiveness Coach, Lifestyle and Habit Change Coach, Narcissists Life Coach, Life Story, etc., because to rewire the mind, repetition is of importance to create a habit in a way of thought. Many of these classes were repetitive and she became aware of that and knowing how her mind worked, she knew hearing the information repeatedly would instill a new program and that's exactly what it did.

Moreover, she now needed to understand her deep-rooted programming, and after experiencing a traumatic event, Nina was able to sit with herself to identify where her programming was rooted. She decided to take some classes and read some books on different belief systems to understand where some of her programming may have come from. Nina then started taking classes on various world religions at Place of Bliss Academy to understand the role religion has on our beliefs and mindsets and that's when she realized the connection between all religions and how some have been used to "control" instead of "enlighten". After that she began studying different ideologies and cultural beliefs to really gain an understanding on how our belief systems and mindsets were formed.

That led her analyzing everything in her life. People, places, things, music, entertainment, school, authority, healthcare, government, and it made her realize how we are programmed by everything we consume. While this was a hard pill to swallow, never fearing a challenge, she decided that she was going to break free from the programming and document every step so that she could pay it forward. After spending most of her life being manipulated, gas lit and lied to by the very people who were supposed to be there for her and love her, Nina developed the amazing ability to identify the very patterns and behaviors of those who manipulate and abuse by using her innate attention to detail and pattern recognition from the very experiences that jaded her life.

During her rewire, not only did she identify the very thoughts, emotions, and behaviors of her own that needed rewiring, but she was able to analyze each situation through memory to understand where her negative programming originated, therefore, giving her a better understanding of how her habitual thoughts and emotions were created in the first place. Through this, she was able to determine how worry and guilt played a major role in how she was programmed followed by fear and a strong victim mentality. She realized that there were significant reasons for her programmed mind and most of them were dictated by worry, guilt, fear, and not feeling valuable.

During her deep dive, she determined that the very negative self-talk was a collection of negative remarks made over time by other people and none of it was actually, even true. The amount of time and energy wasted on listening to that inner critic to only realize that it was wrong and coming from people that did not even have clearance to make comments like that in the first place. Then to realize that these people had an impact on her whole life because she subconsciously held onto the habit of those beliefs for many years. To realize that those people did not even deserve that amount of time in her mind and life was a big eye opener and gave her the ability to change her perceptions once and for all.

Once she started thinking about this, she realized that all of the people she gave credit to for holding her down did not even have the value to make such claims, so why was she letting it impact her for so long? She allowed these moments to create an emotion within her subconscious that immediately went off when negative self-talk started. Furthermore, she realized that she needed to change the habit of how she spoke to herself to clear away these subconsciously programmed emotions.

Nina then started to analyze her thoughts, emotions, and behaviors in real time to understand how her mind and body worked together to create the overall experience. She spent endless hours analyzing her thoughts, emotions, and behaviors to truly understand how it all worked together so that she could figure out how to control her human being by controlling her emotions through how she perceived.

So, after years and years of digging deep, Nina Marie Maldonado was able to rewire her mind, change her mindsets, beliefs systems, and overall perceptions so that she could heal from her past and create the reality of her dreams from the inside out, instead of the outside in. Embrace her authentic self without the boundaries placed on her mind by various forms of programming, Awakening her Mindset, while opening channels for a brighter present moment.

Now, it has become a habitual practice, and she has brought the Awakened Mindset to fruition. In this book, she takes you on the complete journey to the Awakened Mindset through the Programmed Mindset, creating principles from Epistemology to help guide you to an Awakened Mindset, exposing various forms of programming, and in return creating a complete Subconscious Audit System for reprogramming the mind using Mindfulness, Cognitive Behavior Therapy, and Neuro-Linguistic Programming.

Her overall goal is to spread awareness and help other human beings understand their human being. She believes that everyone should embrace their authentic self because everyone is different for a reason and that is to share their individual uniqueness to add to the universal masterpiece, and that alone should be celebrated. Like each stroke of paint on a mural, each placement adds to the beauty and definition to contribute to an overall masterpiece. Embrace your authenticity like each stroke of paint on a mural and add to this beautiful masterpiece that we call reality.

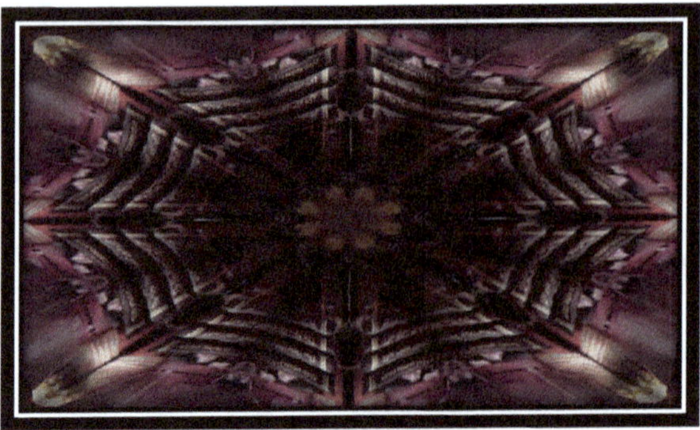

Introduction: Writers Eat for Life

"Writers starve" were the words I was told when I first expressed my motivation to write and express myself after years of just holding in my emotions. *Writers starve?* Confused and bewildered, I thought to myself, *damn, I was just trying to finally find something that I truly enjoyed that I was really, really good at. You know something that was of "my interest" and that made "my heart" flutter.* I remember when I struggled in silence trying to teach myself to read in the bathroom at home after school and between paragraphs in class when the teacher had us read out loud. The pain I would feel as a child because I did not know how to read correctly, and the embarrassment of messing up in front of others crippled me so much as a child that I spent hours on my own, in silence, learning to read so I wouldn't be made fun of.

I remember I used to carry a dictionary and thesaurus around with me so I could understand the words I was reading. In retrospect, I could not understand why the same person who told me, *I can do anything that I put my mind to*, was telling me that the one thing I want to put my mind to is a bad choice. The anger that came over me after finally finding my niche and being told it was pointless and did not have value was a breaking point for me. How hard am I going to keep trying for other people's happiness? For years I never understood why, but finally, I have come to realize. And while I was disappointed for years after that and eventually stopped writing for a good while, I finally understood that it really had no value to me because it was not my belief, it was someone else's belief that I allowed to hinder me.

Unfortunately, I let another person's belief of me change my whole perception. That limited belief of someone else impacted my life for years and only because I did not understand the truth, did I allow it to affect me. If I looked at it differently, I could have lived a much different life. However, I am here to prove to myself that writers don't have to starve and to finally end that limited belief system that always made me question my passions. If I can do it, so can you. You just need to believe. And in this, I am going to tell you how to fix this so you can create the best version of yourself for yourself. Remember, you cannot control anything, but how you let it affect you.

I write today to show that with an understanding and being aware of your thoughts, emotions, and behaviors, you can identify problem areas to resolve any habits that you may have that may not be beneficial for your livelihood. Belief is a habit of a perspective so while many believe certain things, those certain things become a part of your everyday life, they become a part of who you are as an individual, and they pour out through your personality. However, many of our beliefs systems are jaded and they hold us down. We live with them daily and don't even think about them. There are limits in front of us every day, and in today's society, it is even worse. The world thrives on comparison and pain. Quite concerning to say the least.

We are in the era of watching others live instead of living ourselves, constantly comparing ourselves to others and their lives and experiences. We thrive to be a part of something that seems bigger than what it really even needs to be but that is due to external pressures and the need for validation. Our exposure in life, cultures, religions, beliefs, etc., are the pinnacles to our perceptions and until we truly understand how they interconnect and influence each one of us, we will forever be programmed in a system meant to limit us and keep us from our real destinies.

Many of us have a name that is chosen before we are born, so that identity is chosen for you before you even have taken your first breath. We are born into certain demographics with different beliefs, habits, cultures, and ways of living without even knowing what any of this means. So, we grow up inheriting beliefs, behaviors, ideas, and systems that eventually become our identities. We don't question too much when we are younger and if questions were asked, most time, they are disregarded because "we are children and we should not ask questions". "Children should be seen and not heard" was one of the things I remember hearing growing up which became a belief system that led into my adulthood and even implemented in the beginning practices of being a parent myself. In school, if you asked questions, you were told to just listen, in church, if you asked questions about the practices and/or beliefs, you were labeled as a rebel and silenced with fear of being doomed by the almighty god, and if you questioned the government, you're labeled a trader to your nation and your people.

My father was in the service so I remember believing that he was a part of the government's protection so they can't be bad, right? Little did I know the true impact the war had on my father until growing up and being raised by him. He was extremely programmed by the Military and many of the practices taught to me were from the habitual practices in the service that continued throughout his life. From day one, any questions about beliefs and practices were denied recognition. I remember the word "why" being defined as worse than the word "fuck" in my house. We couldn't ask why. The answer was, "because I said so and that's final." We spend the first years of our lives learning to walk and talk, and the rest of our lives being told to sit down and shut the fuck up. Shit, why teach us to talk in the first place? There is a reason. We need to talk so we can learn the program of the systems. We are a part of the larger picture. Welcome to the human condition.

From day one, we are born into a programmed system devised to keep us in certain groups based on mindsets, belief systems, and overall perceptions filtered through each system implemented over time. As we take our first breath, the government is preparing our tags. The tags that will indoctrinate us into a system that will create certain beliefs, habits, and behaviors, to ideally create the identities of people that fit the mold of how they want society to be. Many say we are trapped in a matrix meaning we are trapped in a simulation of reality. I believe that we may be in an established program based on simulated beliefs and systems.

Some of these very systems have been created to keep control and order over the masses by using fear and hate. Being stuck in certain beliefs and systems is usually accompanied by a limited mindset, and that alone can feel like being stuck in a redundant simulation with rules and algorithms controlling how things end up. But really, that could be one's perception of it. Reminds me of a movie I saw many years ago when I was just a child, Groundhog Day, starring Bill Murray. The guy, Phil, a real jerk and narcissist, nonetheless, lived the same day over and over again. I remember being a kid and thinking to myself, what a nightmare. I would never want to experience that. Then I grew up, and life alone became its own Groundhog Day.

A ground hog day of routines and systems that once again resembles that exact nightmare that I recognized as a child. So restricted and limited to never experience another day, a different day. To live something different and experience different things. The point of the matter is, when stuck in limited beliefs with irrational thoughts, impulsive emotions accompanied by tainted behaviors and a fixed identity based on the approval of others, can and will feel like a never-ending Ground Hog Day, "matrixed" lifestyle. And I hate to break it to you, but that is life for many people. The best way to truly fix being in this loop is by becoming aware of your limited belief systems and perceptions.

In retrospect, a belief system is a habit of a perspective, so if you can see things differently, then you can think differently, which will cause you to feel differently, and ultimately, perceive differently, helping to create a new outlook and self. One that can be yours and one that can embrace true authenticity as it is key to finding your true inner peace. I will say this though, by the end of the movie the same day loop was broken and not by coincidence, by transforming who he was as an individual to escape the programmed identity that limited him and held him back, keeping him in that redundant, nightmarish loop.

Speaking of nightmarish loops, my initial path was none other but that very thing. My limited belief systems, victim mentality, and jaded perception led me into a dark place, influencing me to lose my mind for years, to finally one day, just not wanting to be "lost" anymore. I did not like who I had become, and I was determined to change that. I still to this day have no clue where that strength came from.

One day I was toast and then the next day, I just knew I had more to give even if it were just to myself. I was going to become the woman I needed when I was a little girl. I needed to become the woman I needed because I needed some healing, and the only way to help myself was to understand why I was the way I was, where it all came from, and how to rearrange and organize it, because it was in a pile on the floor in a mess, and I couldn't find anything. While I was trying to seek approval from everyone else and trying to save everyone else, I lost myself, and no one was coming to save me, so I had to save myself. And that's just what I did.

We start our lives, and we are around certain people from day one that will influence the rest of our lives, and we really have no choice in the option. But, perhaps, maybe we do have a choice after all. Maybe that choice is to examine our "systems" and see what is working and what is not. Perhaps, the only thing standing in our way is our own perception. So, with that being said, let's rewrite this timeline because this story is redundant and played out. It's time to change our minds for the better of our present days and futures. Writers don't starve in my story; they eat for life. Let's shine. Change your Mind, Change your Life.

"At "The Awakened Mindset: The Epistemic Ripple Effect," I believe in the inherent power of every mind to heal and grow.

I decode the negative programming that holds us back – from fear to consumerism – and offer you the blueprints to construct a resilient Knowledge Architecture.

Together, we embark on a journey of mental awakening, igniting an Epistemic Ripple Effect that spreads outwards, healing hearts and building a world where clarity and compassion prevail, uniting us all.

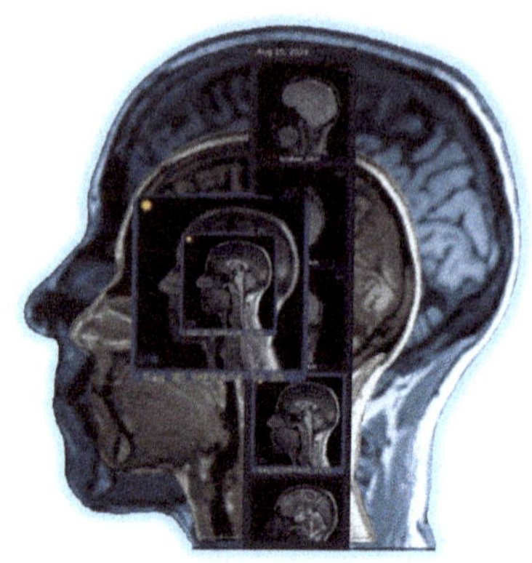

Part 1
The Human Condition

We are born, we are given a name, birth certificates, a social security number and card, we are now legal. We can live. We are born into families, belief systems, cultures, religions, ideologies, therefore, many of our personalities and identities form from things that existed before we even did. So, if you really think about it, we are all made up of other people, places, and things that we truly don't even know so much about or even fully understand until they are already ingrained into our systems. This is where I found myself while I was in the beginning of the reprogramming journey.

My programming, just like many others, was and in some ways is still deeply rooted. To accurately reprogram your mind, you need to know the root of where this programming originated to understand how to change it. Moreover, I have spent endless hours studying my mind, my thoughts, my emotions, my behaviors, consciousness, and subconscious, so that I could understand how I was programmed throughout the years and how to change my perceptions to reprogram my mind. And that's really it; that's the key to most of this, changing your perception and how you see life.

Life has been painted for us throughout the years through the lens of others and their experiences, our experiences, and how we individually perceive each particular experience. That's right, the bearer of bad news is here, but we all have different perceptions. We are designed to be different through our makeup. Not one of us has the same DNA exactly, so why would we be exactly alike? We will never be. The design does not call for it. Each one of us rarely shares the same exact perception because of the way we individually perceive. However, we often latch onto the perceptions of others. We only do that when we believe in something we are programmed to believe, which respectfully, is the majority of society, myself, included. To realize we are all part of a system was a big pill to swallow. However, it gave me the awareness that I needed to change my perception and awaken my mindset.

The system I am referring to is what I call the "Mental Matrix". Often invisible, the Mental Matrix is a framework of assumptions and limitations. Our deeply ingrained beliefs and mindsets can create a Mental Matrix, a system of limitations that shape our perception of reality and our potential. In order to break free from the Mental Matrix and its limitations on your perceptions and abilities, it is important to cultivate an Awakened Mindset, one of critical thinking, reason, empathy, and compassion, to change the way in which we perceive reality and our overall perceptions of the world.

Chapter 1

Understanding the System:
Your Mind,
Your Programming,
Your Reality

1. Knowledge Architecture:
Your Personal Structure of Knowledge

Your knowledge architecture is the network of beliefs, values, and experiences that shapes how you see the world. Think of it as your personal "operating system", the unique lens through which you interpret every piece of data you encounter. This isn't just a collection of facts; it's the individualized structure of your memories and interpretations. It's the product of everything you've learned and processed, whether you realize it or not. Ultimately, this architecture is the blueprint of your reality. Because this system dictates your every perception, keeping it organized and critically examined is the only way to build a truly healthy mindset and lifestyle.

2. Mindset: The Foundation of Your Being

Your mindset is the "operating system" of your consciousness, the foundational framework that dictates how you interpret reality, navigate challenges, and perceive your own potential. Much like the lens of a camera, it determines what you focus on and how you frame the world around you. While it functions as your default mental setting, it is important to recognize that this internal framework is rarely a product of conscious choice. From birth, our mindsets are shaped by a complex web of external programming and ingrained belief systems. They are not monolithic or fixed; rather, they are built from the "habits of our perspective." Because your mindset was formed through a process of accumulation, it can be dismantled and reconstructed through conscious awareness. The first step toward transformation is not simply "thinking differently," but understanding the architecture of how your current beliefs were built. By identifying these core components, you shift from being a passive user of your mental operating system to its active programmer.

3. Belief Systems: The Fundamental Convictions that Shape Your Mindset

If your mindset is your overarching mental attitude, your belief systems are the specific convictions that give it shape and substance. Beliefs are the individual "lines of code" or building blocks you hold to be true about yourself and the world. Collectively, these convictions form your mindset. When these internal codes are limited, they create a "fixed" mindset that hinders growth and limits potential. Therefore, auditing these fundamental beliefs is the first step toward awakening your perspective; after all, we do not see the world as it is, but through the filter our beliefs have constructed through our emotions.

4. Perception:
The Reality You Construct (Emotional Reality)

To perceive is the act of gathering data; to have a perception is the result of that data being processed. This distinction is vital because the way we interpret sensory information, what we see, hear, and feel, directly constructs the reality we inhabit. We rarely experience the world in its raw state; instead, our ingrained belief systems act as a cognitive filter. This "lens" automatically colors and distorts information before it ever reaches our conscious mind. Consequently, the world we "see" is less an objective truth and more a reflection of our internal convictions. This raises a critical question, how exactly are these hidden scripts dictating our version of reality?

5. Reality: Physical (Objective) and Emotional (Subjective) Reality

What we call "reality" is actually a dual experience. First, there is physical reality, the objective, external world that exists regardless of our awareness. If a storm is passing through, the rain is a constant, unchangeable fact. However, parallel to this is emotional reality, the internal landscape formed by our beliefs, mindsets, biases, and history. While physical reality provides the raw material, emotional reality is the processor. Two people can stand in the same downpour; one finds it "miserable and depressing," while the other finds it "cozy and romantic." The rain is objective, but the experience is a personal creation. We often fall into the trap of attributing our internal state to external events, claiming "that person made me feel this way", when, in fact, the emotion is a product of our own internal filters. Recognizing this distinction is the key to psychological agency. It is the shift from viewing your feelings as inevitable reactions to understanding them as subjective interpretations.

Chapter 2

Cultivating an Awakened Mindset

1. Epistemology: The Study of Knowledge

Epistemology is the formal study of knowledge, traditionally defined as Justified True Belief. Rather than a static discovery, it is an evolving framework developed by philosophers to answer a deceptively simple question, how do we know what we know? It investigates the nature of truth, the limits of human understanding, and the rigorous standards required to validate a claim. But how do we determine if a belief is truly "justified"? Justification acts as the bridge between a lucky guess and actual knowledge. We build this bridge using several key sources:

- Perception: Data gathered through our physical senses.
- Reason: The application of logic and innate rational ideas.
- Testimony: Knowledge passed to us by others and external records.
- Memory: The retrieval of past experiences and data.
- Introspection: The observation of our own internal mental states.
- Intuition: Immediate insights that occur without conscious reasoning.

While these sources provide the foundation for our convictions, epistemology also demands a layer of healthy skepticism. Understanding these mechanisms allows us to critically audit our most deeply ingrained beliefs, forcing us to ask whether our "truths" are built on solid evidence or merely comfortable assumptions.

2. Epistemic Principles:

Developing Your Epistemic Compass using Principles for True Knowing

Before we dive into the specific Epistemic Principles that will guide your journey, it is vital to understand why these principles are the bedrock of the Awakened Mindset. As we have explored, epistemology is the vast philosophical study of knowledge, how we acquire it, what makes it true, and how we justify our beliefs. But how do we apply such a grand discipline to the deeply personal work of uncovering and reprogramming the subconscious? The answer lies in distilling that grand inquiry into actionable, internal commitments.

Our minds are often running on old, inherited, or culturally imposed "programming." This has created a Knowledge Architecture that prioritizes conformity, comfort, and survival over genuine understanding. This architecture leads to jaded perceptions and limits our ability to see the truth clearly. To break free from this "Mental Matrix," information alone is not enough; we require a new way of knowing. We must cultivate intellectual virtues, a new internal compass that actively guides us toward reliable, authentic knowledge and away from the gravity of unconsciously accepted beliefs.

From philosophy to practice, these Epistemic Principles for the Awakened Mindset are not abstract philosophical concepts to be debated in academic circles. Instead, they are distilled from epistemology, they draw from the foundational questions of epistemology, such as the need for justification, critical examination, and understanding our own cognitive limits. These principles are specifically tailored for reprogramming. They have been selected and adapted to address the unique psychological friction of confronting deeply ingrained subconscious patterns. The goal is to empower you to question not just *what* you believe, but *how* you came to believe it. In doing so, you move away from rigid, external rules and toward fluid, actionable virtues.

By intentionally practicing these principles, you transform your relationship with knowledge itself. You cease to be a passive vessel for cultural and inherited programming and become an active architect. You learn to discern, evaluate, and consciously build a Knowledge Architecture that serves your highest good and aligns with a more objective reality.

As you embark on your Subconscious Audit, these principles will serve as your inner guide. They provide the scaffolding you need to remain courageous, honest, and open-minded while exploring the hidden corners of your mind. This is the framework upon which you will build your Awakened Mindset.

3. The Epistemic Ripple Effect:
The Epistemic Principles for Awakening Your Mindset

- **Intellectual Humility:** Recognizing the limits of your own knowledge and being open to the possibility of being wrong. It involves acknowledging biases and being willing to learn from others. Admitting when you don't know something and being receptive to new information, even if it contradicts your current beliefs.

- **Intellectual Courage:** The willingness to critically examine beliefs, especially those that are widely held or emotionally charged, and to stand up for what you believe is true, even if it's unpopular. Questioning long-held societal norms or challenging misinformation even when it's uncomfortable.

- **Intellectual Autonomy:** Thinking for yourself, forming your own reasoned judgments, and not being unduly dependent on the opinions of others. Researching different perspectives on an issue and forming your own conclusion rather than blindly following what others say.

- **Intellectual Empathy:** Understanding and appreciating the perspectives of others, even when you disagree with them. It involves actively listening to and trying to understand the reasoning behind someone else's belief, even if you find it flawed.

- **Intellectual Integrity:** Holding yourself to the same rigorous standards of evidence and reasoning that you expect from others. It involves being honest and consistent in your pursuit of knowledge. Acknowledging when your own arguments are weak or when new evidence contradicts your previous conclusions.

- **Fair-mindedness:** Considering all relevant viewpoints impartially, without prejudice, and being open to changing your mind when presented with compelling evidence. Giving equal consideration to arguments from different political ideologies or perspectives on a controversial topic.

- **Open-mindedness:** Being receptive to new ideas and information, even if they challenge your existing beliefs. It involves a willingness to consider possibilities that you may not have previously entertained. Being willing to listen to and learn about different cultures or ways of life, even if they are very different from your own.

- **Skepticism:** Owning a questioning attitude towards claims and not accepting them at face value. It involves seeking evidence and reasons to support beliefs. Asking for evidence or sources when someone makes a strong claim and being wary of unsubstantiated assertions.

- **Confidence in Reason:** Trusting in the power of logic and evidence to lead to sound conclusions. It involves believing that reasoned inquiry is the best way to understand the world. Relying on logical arguments and factual data when making decisions or forming opinions.

- **Intellectual Perseverance:** Being willing to grapple with complex issues and not giving up easily when faced with challenges in the pursuit of knowledge. Spending the time and effort needed to understand a difficult concept or to thoroughly research a complex topic.

4. The Awakened Mindset:
The Conscious Awakening

What is an Awakened Mindset? An Awakened Mindset is a state of active and conscious engagement with your own thoughts, beliefs, and the world around you. It's a dynamic and evolved way of being that moves beyond passively accepting pre-programmed ideas and instead embraces critical thinking, self-awareness, empathy, and the power of conscious choice in shaping your inner mental landscape. Traits of an Awakened Mindset include:

- Actively seeking, processing, and critically analyzing and evaluating information.
- Reflective and critical when questioning assumptions and consistently searching for a deeper understanding.
- Internally guided by personal values, reasoned judgment, and conscious choice.
- Embodies extreme self-awareness of personal biases, thought and behavior patterns, and the influence of shaping beliefs.
- Consciously open and fair minded, influencing consideration of diverse perspectives and allows for one's ability to question and challenge one's own assumptions.
- High sense of personal agency proactively shapes thoughts, beliefs, and behaviors, allowing for adaptation and resilience in the face of challenges.
- Driven by intrinsic motivation, personal growth, and core values.
- More conscious and intentional: actively engages with thoughts (metacognition) and the world.

An Awakened Mindset is more conscious and aware of its engagement with oneself and the world. In a world where authenticity is a lost art, cultivating an Awakened Mindset can help each of us find our true self without the filters implemented by external forces. But how does one find lost art? By digging deep. Just as archaeologists meticulously excavate ancient ruins, or art restorers carefully chip away centuries of grime, we too must dig deep to rediscover our lost art of authenticity. This "digging deep" begins in your subconscious.

As you dig deeper, you begin to reveal the contours of your original, unblemished self. You rediscover innate wisdom, forgotten desires, and an inherent worth that was always there, simply waiting to be seen. This isn't only about embracing a new self but remembering and restoring the masterpiece that already exists.

The journey of the Awakened Mindset is therefore an archaeological expedition into the self. It's the courageous act of digging through the layers of programming and jaded perceptions to unearth your most precious possession, your authentic self. And in doing so, you don't just transform your own life; you reveal a piece of the universal human masterpiece, contributing to the "*Epistemic Ripple* Effect" and inspiring others to embark on their own profound excavations.

5. Subconscious Mind:
The Vast, Hidden information

When we use the metaphor of "digging deep" to find the "lost art" of authenticity, we are very specifically referring to the act of engaging with, exploring, and ultimately transforming your subconscious mind. This isn't just a figure of speech; it describes the precise domain where profound change occurs. Think of your subconscious mind as the place we store all our memories based on experiences, deeply ingrained habits and automated patterns, and our fundamental beliefs about ourselves and the world. It's our automatic emotional responses and even our hidden motivations and protective mechanisms.

Most of these exist and act without conscious thought or effort and influence your everyday perceptions. Intentionally engaging with your subconscious, the vast reservoir where your programming resides, the messages, lessons, fears, and assumptions that were absorbed through life, can help you understand the programming that affects how you perceive yourself and the world around you. The subconscious stores, processes, and applies information and knowledge to form your overall perception of reality.

But what if the information and knowledge we store for later processing and application is faulty, jaded, and immensely limited and fixed? What happens then?

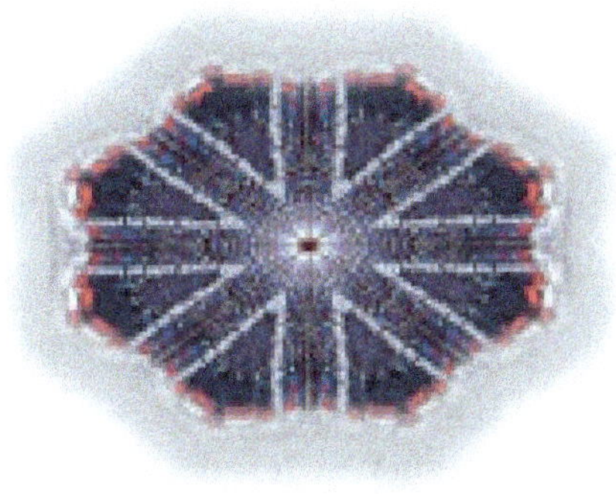

Chapter 3

The Prison Program

1. Programmed Mindset:

The Subconscious Prison

Imagine a prisoner in a cell. We typically envision iron bars, concrete walls, and locked doors. But what if the most insidious prison is not made of steel and stone, but of thought and perception? This is the reality of a programmed mindset; it creates a Subconscious Prison. This prison is not a physical place you can see or touch; it is an internal constraint, built by the very mechanisms of your subconscious mind operating on ingrained programming. It is a subtle, yet immensely powerful, confinement that dictates your reality, often without your conscious awareness.

Invisible walls of belief, bars of automated patterns and habits, guarded by fear and resistance, influence limited perceptions, lack of genuine choice, repetitive cycles, and unfulfilled potential. The crazier part of all this is that usually the "prisoner" often does not even realize that their mind has been "incarcerated". Due to limited beliefs and perceptions, the assumption that reality is meant to be limited becomes reality. In retrospect, the programmed mindset is a Subconscious Prison of limitations.

Traits of a programmed mindset include one who:

- Accepts information without significant questioning,
- Largely influenced by external forces.
- Beliefs that are often accepted without examination, due to a limited understanding of personal biases and the origins of belief.
- Narrow and fixed perspective that is very resistant to alternative viewpoints.
- Often focused on external validation, societal expectations, and material possessions contributes to a low sense of agency influencing a victim mentality.
- Automative and unconscious and operates on autopilot based on ingrained beliefs.

As a result, the bars have been woven into the fabric of the mind so deeply that reality is shaped based on their limited beliefs and perceptions which keep one in a programmed state of mind. Realistically, the Subconscious Prison was not built alone, it took a complex web of interconnected thoughts, beliefs, expectations, biases, and assumptions to form this prison.

2. The Mental Matrix:
The Infrastructure of Your Subconscious Prison

Our ingrained beliefs and mindsets create a "Mental Matrix", a system of limitations that shapes our perception of reality and our potential. If the programmed mindset is the Subconscious Prison, then the Mental Matrix is its intricate, invisible architecture and operating system. It's the complex web of interconnected thoughts, beliefs, expectations, biases, and assumptions that the subconscious mind constantly references and processes to construct your individual reality. The Mental Matrix is the master blueprint or the system of interconnected neural pathways and associations within your subconscious mind.

You did not necessarily design this blueprint; it was largely "downloaded" or "installed" through various forms of programming from your environment, your family, culture, education, media, and significant life experiences. It includes all the "rules" your subconscious follows about safety, value, love, success, failure, and the very nature of existence. Moreover, the Mental Matrix is a restricted system of mindsets and beliefs that govern our thoughts and behaviors, keeping us with a limited and fixed perspective about ourselves, the world, and the possibilities that both have to offer. The Mental Matrix as the infrastructure of the Subconscious Prison consists of the prison walls (limiting beliefs) and the prison bars (automated responses).

The Mental Matrix builds the walls of your Subconscious Prison by solidifying limited beliefs. These beliefs then function as boundaries and dictate what you perceive about yourself and the world. In return, the interconnect patterns within the Mental Matrix create automated responses, habits, and emotional triggers that function like prison bars. Your subconscious, following the matrix's established pathways, leads you to react in predictable ways, even if those ways are unhelpful or self-sabotaging. Furthermore, the reality you perceive is projected by your Mental Matrix. You see what your Mental Matrix is programmed to show you by reinforcing the illusion that its confines are only truth and by making you believe that its boundaries are the world's boundaries. The Mental Matrix is simply a programmed, limited know

-ledge architecture.

Recognizing the Mental Matrix as the architecture of your Subconscious Prison is the first step towards liberation. It reveals that the limitations you experience are not inherent truths about you or the world, but rather the result of an internal system that can be understood, examined, and reprogrammed. The "digging deep" of the Subconscious Audit is precisely the work of dissecting this Mental Matrix, identifying its faulty programming, and consciously rebuilding it to serve your authentic self and awakened perception.

3. Worried Mindset:
The Thief in Your Mind

"Worried about the thief in your pocket, better worry about the thief in your mind." Most of us are vigilant about external threats to our well-being, securing our homes, protecting our valuables, avoiding physical dangers. But how often do we recognize the internal thief that operates within our own minds?

The Worried Mindset is precisely a programmed internal intruder that robs you of your mental and emotional freedom. Having just explored the Mental Matrix as the very architecture of your Subconscious Prison, a programmed, limited knowledge architecture, it is time to examine one of its most insidious inhabitants, the Worried Mindset. This mindset is not just an occasional concern; it is a deeply ingrained pattern of thought and perception that can silently steal your peace, potential, and presence. It is a habitual pattern of focusing on potential negative outcomes, rehearsing worst-case scenarios, and constantly anticipating threats, even when there is no immediate danger. It's a state of chronic apprehension, often fueled by excessive "what ifs", a relentless loop of questioning future possibilities, almost always leading to a negative conclusion.

It's catastrophizing such as blowing small concerns out of proportion and imagining the absolute worst possible results. Thus, contributing to rumination and getting stuck in repetitive thought patterns about past events or future uncertainties without moving towards solutions, and a need for control through an often-futile attempt to mentally control uncontrollable future events by overthinking them. This is not about healthy planning or problem-solving; it's about a mind caught in a cycle of unproductive, often debilitating, anxiety.

The Worried Mindset is not an accidental visitor; it's a direct product of the Mental Matrix, and thus, a powerful example of programming in action. Often installed through programming like early experiences, growing up in an environment where worry was prevalent, or where safety felt uncertain. This can hardwire your subconscious to be constantly on alert and to worry as a sign of responsibility or care. "If you're not worrying, you're not trying hard enough". Negative reinforcement, if worrying about a remote possibility (like forgetting your keys) leads to you checking them constantly, and a perceived negative outcome (losing them) doesn't occur, your subconscious might falsely attribute your safety to the act of worrying, reinforcing the behavior. Once this "worry program" is embedded in your Mental Matrix, your subconscious mind treats it as a standard operating procedure. It utilizes its incredible processing power not to solve problems, but to efficiently generate and run scenarios of potential threats.

Your knowledge architecture, the structure of your Mental Matrix, becomes organized around anticipating danger. Every piece of information that enters your perception is unconsciously filtered. By constantly focusing on what might go wrong, the Worried Mindset robs you of the present moment calm, joy, and contentment. Your mind is always in the future, anticipating trouble. When you are lost in worry, you're not actively engaged with what's happening now. Conversations, experiences, and beauty pass by unnoticed because your attention is fixated on internal anxieties. The energy consumed by worrying is energy diverted from creative thinking, problem-solving, and decisive action.

It can lead to analysis paralysis, preventing you from pursuing opportunities or making necessary changes. Your mind is so busy running worry scripts that it can't execute growth programs. The Worried Mindset acts as a powerful distortion field within your Mental Matrix. It ensures that your overall perception of yourself and the world is perpetually tinged with anxiety. You might perceive neutral events as threats, genuine feedback as criticism, or opportunities as overwhelming risks. Your reality becomes a constant potential danger zone. The Worried Mindset, therefore, is a prime example of how a programmed aspect of your Mental Matrix can create a subtle, yet pervasive, internal prison. Recognizing this thief and understanding its origins in your programming is a vital step toward reclaiming your mind and your life.

4. Guilt Programming:
The Internal Accuser

If the Worried Mindset is the thief that steals your peace by constantly anticipating external threats, then Guilt Programming is the relentless inner accuser, constantly reminding you that you are not, have not, or will not be enough. It's a deeply uncomfortable feeling of self-blame, self-reproach, or unworthiness, often triggered by faint cues and operating in the background of your consciousness. Guilt Programming is a deeply embedded pattern within your subconscious mind that causes you to habitually experience feelings of guilt, shame, or inadequacy.

Unlike a healthy sense of remorse which leads to corrective action, programmed guilt is often disproportionate, it's out of sync with the actual "offense" which might be none at all, or a minor perceived shortcoming. It is persistent; it lingers long after any reasonable need for self-correction has passed, and it is pervasive in its nature as it can attach itself to a wide range of situations, from not being productive enough to simply resting or enjoying yourself. Thus, resulting in self-punishing behavior, keeping you locked in a cycle of self-criticism rather than motivating positive change.

This program ensures you remain in a state of internal discomfort, often driving over-effort, people-pleasing, or self-sabotage. Guilt Programming, like the Worried Mindset, is a powerful manifestation of your Mental Matrix in action, directly shaped by past programming. This program is often installed through early childhood experiences where love or approval felt conditional, tied to performance, obedience, or self-sacrifice. Messages like "You're only good if you try harder," "Don't be selfish," or "You should feel bad for that" lay the groundwork of how one stays in this programmed loop.

Most cultures and religions have strong emphasis on guilt as a moral compass, which can be beneficial in moderation, but can also lead to excessive self-blame and a belief that inherent human nature is flawed. If you were held to impossibly ambitious standards, or absorbed a belief that perfection is the only acceptable outcome, your subconscious learned to generate guilt whenever you inevitably fall short. The Mental Matrix runs the "Guilt Program".

Once embedded, your Mental Matrix uses its powerful processing capabilities to diligently execute the "Guilt Program." When you try to rest, relax, or simply be, the matrix might automatically trigger thoughts like, "You haven't earned this rest," "There's so much more you should be doing," or "Someone else needs your help more." This program dictates how your Mental Matrix processes self-evaluation. Your subconscious is programmed to constantly look for evidence of your inadequacies, ensuring the feeling of guilt remains present. Guilt Programming, this inner accuser, profoundly impacts your perception and overall well-being.

By constantly highlighting perceived failures or shortcomings, guilt erodes your inherent sense of self-worth. You begin to *perceive* yourself as inherently flawed or never "enough," regardless of your actual achievements or efforts. The experience of guilt often prevents you from fully enjoying successes, relaxation, or personal desires. There's always an underlying sense of "I don't deserve this" or "I should be doing something else." Programmed guilt can compel you into overworking, people-pleasing, or self-sacrificing behaviors, not from genuine desire, but from a desperate attempt to quiet the inner accuser.

Conversely, it can also lead to paralysis, where the fear of not doing "enough" prevents you from doing anything at all. This program makes you *perceive* your own efforts as constantly insufficient. Even when you've given your all, the guilt program in your Mental Matrix will highlight the imagined areas where you "could have done more," ensuring you never truly feel satisfied or accomplished. Just as the Worried Mindset is a thief that anticipates loss, guilt programming is an inner accuser that demands continuous payment for perceived debts that may not even exist.

Recognizing this constant inner voice, how it functions within your Mental Matrix, and where its programming originated, is essential to dismantling this emotional prison.

5. The Imperfection Trap:
The Programming of Fundamental Flawed

The Imperfection Trap is a profoundly ingrained program within your Mental Matrix that operates on the core belief that you are fundamentally flawed, tainted by past mistakes, and therefore inherently unworthy of true pride, unconditional love, or significant public recognition. It's a self-perpetuating cycle where any perceived deviation from an impossible standard of perfection triggers intense self-judgment and guilt, effectively suppressing authentic self-expression and preventing genuine self-acceptance.

The imprinted standard of perfection is installed through early experiences, often involving contradictory messages or a constant emphasis on flawlessness. For instance, trying to make your parent proud, but they are never satisfied, so in the long run, you never feel satisfied. It sets an unattainable benchmark for your actions, achievements, and even your very being. Crucially, the trap is cemented by specific, often traumatic, events that are interpreted by your developing subconscious as "proof" of your inherent unworthiness.

A single negative outcome following a moment of pride is catastrophized into universal evidence that your independent success inevitably leads to failure or negative consequences. The moment you feel pride, confidence, or the urge to "boast" by expressing authentic self-worth, this program triggers a powerful wave of guilt.

This guilt isn't rational; it's an automated internal mechanism designed to punish you for straying from the "flawed" self-concept. It directly ties into Guilt Programming. Therefore, expressing pride or confident self-advocacy is linked to potential negative outcomes, the trap compels you to minimize your achievements, downplay your strengths, and avoid notoriety. This manifests as suppressed self-expression and a persistent feeling of "having nothing to brag about," regardless of your actual accomplishments.

This trap often co-exists with intense Performance Pressure. You are driven to achieve, but the "perfection" standard is always just out of reach. Even when you succeed, the internal program immediately devalues it, either by finding a flaw or by triggering the guilt associated with "being better than others," ensuring you never truly feel accomplished. The "Imperfection Trap" can feed a preexisting Victim Mentality, where you subconsciously believe you are destined for setbacks or don't "deserve" unadulterated success, thus perpetuating cycles of self-sabotage.

The Imperfection Trap is a formidable wall within your Subconscious Prison. It keeps you confined by turning your own potential for pride and authentic self-expression into a source of anxiety and self-censorship. It convinces you that your inherent essence is flawed, thereby undermining your capacity to embrace your true power and share your unique, valuable message with the world.

6. The Monkey Mind:
The Restless Engine of Your Prison

We've examined how the Worried Mindset steals your peace by constantly projecting fear into the future, and how Guilt Programming acts as an inner accuser, eroding your self-worth. Now, let's shine a light on the frantic, often chaotic, force that so often fuels both patterns, the Monkey Mind. This term, rooted in ancient Buddhist teachings, perfectly describes a mind that is restless, unsettled, easily distracted, and constantly jumping from thought to thought, much like a monkey leaping erratically from branch to branch. It's the incessant internal chatter, the mind's inability to settle, focus, or simply be in the present moment.

The Monkey Mind isn't just a nuisance; it's a vital component of your Mental Matrix that actively enables and amplifies the effects of the Worried Mindset and Guilt Programming. It's the constant motion that prevents stillness, the noise that drowns out clarity, and the restlessness that prevents deep, conscious engagement. The Monkey Mind thrives on "what ifs." Its very nature is to jump from one possibility to the next, often without a logical conclusion. This provides the perfect environment for the Worried Mindset to flourish. Each mental leap can land on a new potential problem, a new disaster scenario, or a new insecurity.

When your mind is constantly hopping, it struggles to anchor itself in the present moment or to objectively assess reality. This absence of grounding allows fears and anxieties to proliferate unchecked, making it difficult to discern between a real threat and an imagined one. The monkey finds a new "fear branch" to swing to with every passing thought. The Monkey Mind's tendency to loop and ruminate means that once a worry enters, it's not easily let go. It's replayed, analyzed, and intensified, ensuring the "thief in your mind" gets ample opportunity to steal your peace.

The Monkey Mind's incessant chatter often includes a strong component of self-criticism. This restless self-talk acts as a powerful loudspeaker for your Guilt Programming, constantly replaying narratives of perceived inadequacy, past mistakes, or missed opportunities. Just as it struggles to let go of worries, the Monkey Mind also struggles to release thoughts of guilt. It jumps back to perceived shortcomings, re-examines past actions, and constantly compares your efforts to impossible standards, ensuring the inner accuser remains active and loud. The sheer volume and speed of the Monkey Mind's thoughts can prevent you from cultivating a more compassionate inner dialogue. There's no space for stillness, reflection, or the gentle acceptance needed to counter programmed guilt.

Ultimately, the Monkey Mind is another sophisticated mechanism within your Mental Matrix that helps maintain the Subconscious Prison. By keeping you constantly distracted and mentally agitated, the Monkey Mind prevents you from truly observing the walls of your prison, let alone finding the keys. It ensures you're too busy with internal noise to notice the underlying programming that dictates your experience. It pulls you away from the present moment, which is the only place where genuine awareness, intentional choice, and effective reprogramming can occur. If you're always jumping to the past (guilt) or the future (worry), you're never fully here to consciously engage with your inner world.

The Monkey Mind, therefore, is not merely a symptom of modern life; it's an ingrained pattern within your programmed knowledge architecture that actively reinforces your subconscious confinement. Recognizing its relentless activity and understanding how it fuels worry and guilt is a critical step in gaining mastery over your mind and liberating your authentic self.

7. Stolen Focus:
The Ultimate Robbery

We've illuminated the Monkey Mind as the relentless, chattering engine within your Mental Matrix, fueling anxiety and guilt. This restless inner activity isn't just uncomfortable; it actively works to undermine one of your most precious cognitive resources, your focus. This leads us directly to the experience of stolen focus; therefore, the Monkey Mind is the chief thief of focus.

The Monkey Mind, by its very nature of jumping erratically from thought to thought, past regret to future anxiety, directly steals your ability to concentrate on what really matters. Its incessant internal noise prevents you from settling your attention on a single task, a meaningful conversation, a lesson, or even just the simple beauty of the present moment. It's like trying to listen to a whisper in a room full of shouting voices, the signal gets lost in the noise. Every time your mind leaps from your current task to a worry about tomorrow, a regret about yesterday, or a fleeting impulse to check your phone, your focus is fragmented, stolen in micro-moments that accumulate into significant loss.

The consequences of this internal theft are profound, contributing significantly to your experience within the Subconscious Prison. It makes sustained, high-quality work nearly impossible, robbing you of the ability to complete tasks effectively and achieve your goals. True learning requires sustained attention to absorb, process, and integrate new information. Stolen focus makes it difficult to deeply engage with new concepts, hindering your intellectual and personal growth. When your focus is stolen, you are pulled away from the richness of the present moment, you miss deep connection with loved ones, the beauty of your surroundings, and the simple joys of being alive. You are physically present but mentally absent. A scattered mind struggles to think clearly, analyze situations effectively, or make well-reasoned decisions. The path forward remains obscured by the mental fog of distraction.

Ironically, the very act of "digging deep" requires focus. If your attention is constantly fragmented, it's incredibly difficult to observe your own thoughts, emotions, and underlying programming, thus reinforcing the Subconscious Prison. Stolen focus keeps you disoriented within your Subconscious Prison. You're constantly bumping into its invisible walls, unable to see the escape routes, because your attention is too scattered to perceive them clearly. The good news is that focus, unlike a physical possession, can be reclaimed. The antidote to Stolen Focus is the cultivation of Deep Focus, the ability to intentionally direct and sustain your attention on a single task, thought, or experience, free from internal and external distractions. This intentional act of reclaiming your focus is not just a productivity hack; it's a profound act of mental liberation. It's how you begin to gain mastery over your own mind, allowing you to clearly see the architecture of your Mental Matrix, discern the programming, and begin the deliberate work of rewriting your reality. Reclaiming your focus is a key to unlocking the doors of your Subconscious Prison and stepping into an awakened state.

"The Awakened Mindset:
The Epistemic Ripple Effect" is on a mission to illuminate the hidden programming that can cloud our minds with fear, hate, and division.

I empower you to re-architect your inner world, brick by mindful brick, with the solid foundations of knowledge, reason, and compassion.

By cultivating an Awakened Mindset, we can create an Epistemic Ripple effect that washes over our world, building bridges of understanding and fostering a future united in wisdom and peace.

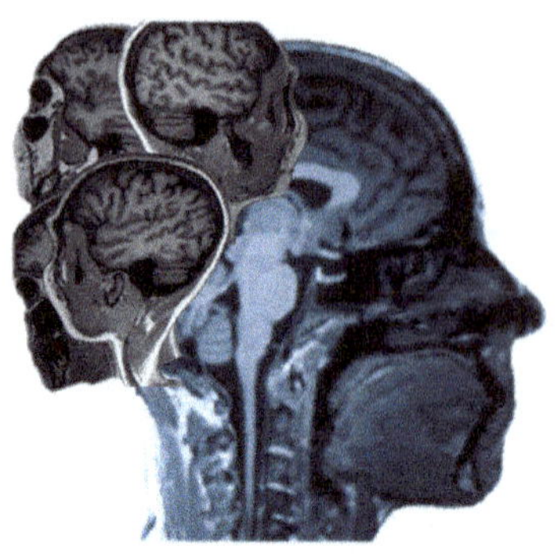

Part 2
The Program

Chapter 4

Everything Down to Your Core Comes from Something Before

Having explored "The Human Condition" and the deeply personal nature of your programmed mindset as a Subconscious Prison, a structure largely built by your Mental Matrix, we now turn our attention to one of the most potent and insidious mechanisms of that confinement, Stolen Focus.

While we initially examined Stolen Focus as a byproduct of your internal Monkey Mind, the restless engine that scatters your attention, we must now acknowledge a darker truth. The theft of your focus is not solely an accidental internal phenomenon; it is a meticulously engineered, often intentional, process used to maintain and amplify the very fear, hate, and division that fragments our collective reality.

1. The Insidious Nature of Stolen Focus: Why Your Attention is the Ultimate Prize

If your attention is your most valuable currency, then its theft is the ultimate robbery. In our modern world, focus is not just lost; it is systematically siphoned away by forces that understand its power. They know that a mind with scattered, fragmented, or stolen focus is a mind unable to critically think, deeply connect, or perceive reality objectively.

Your focus is relentlessly targeted because it prevents critical thinking. A mind constantly flitting from one stimuli to the next lacks the sustained attention necessary to analyze, question, or deeply understand complex issues. When you can't focus, you can't honestly think, making you highly susceptible to simplistic narratives, misinformation, and emotional appeals.

It hampers discernment by making it difficult to distinguish between truth and falsehood, fact and opinion, or genuine concern and manufactured outrage. Nuance is lost, and black-and-white thinking prevails. A fragmented mind is often a stressed and overstimulated mind. When your focus is constantly pulled in multiple directions, you become more emotionally reactive, prone to anger, frustration, and anxiety.

This heightened emotional state makes you fertile ground for messages designed to trigger fear or hatred. By controlling what captures your attention and what doesn't, these forces can dictate your perception of reality. They can amplify certain narratives while muting others, ensuring you see the world through a specific, often divisive, lens.

2. The Mechanisms of This Grand Theft: The Initial Trap

This theft of focus is orchestrated through powerful, often invisible; mechanisms embedded within our daily lives. Digital overload and notification culture, your phone, designed for maximum engagement, constantly pings, vibrates, and alerts you, training your brain to switch tasks and never fully settle. Each notification is a tiny "theft" of your attention.

Algorithmic design of platforms, such as social media, news feeds, and content platforms, are engineered by algorithms that prioritize "engagement" above all else. They learn what triggers your emotions (especially anger, fear, and outrage) and feed you an endless stream of content designed to hook your attention, often sacrificing truth and nuance for clicks and views.

Echo chambers and filter bubbles are used to steal your focus. The algorithms further trap your focus within curated echo chambers. By only showing you content that confirms your existing biases, they reinforce your programmed beliefs, preventing exposure to diverse perspectives and making it harder to connect with those outside your "bubble." Sensationalized and fear-based news cycles are used as emotional triggers to steal your focus, driven by the attention economy, often prioritize sensationalism, conflict, and fearmongering.

This constant barrage of alarming headlines and divisive stories hijacks your focus and keeps your nervous system in a perpetual state of alert, making you more prone to anxiety and tribalism. Alongside the fear, there's an overwhelming volume of trivial, distracting content that drowns out important issues, critical thinking, and opportunities for meaningful connection. It's the ultimate "bread and circuses" scenario, keeping the masses occupied and disengaged from substantive thought.

3. The Consequence:
The Fabrication of Fear, Hate, and Division

The result of this widespread, insidious theft of focus is a society increasingly defined by what I call the 4 D's for creating fear, hate, and division. When focus is stolen, the conditions become ripe for the propagation of fear, hate, and division. A distracted mind cannot fully assess risks. It becomes hyper-vigilant and susceptible to exaggerated threats, whether economic, social, or existential. Fear is a primal emotion that shuts down rational thought and promotes obedience or panic.

When nuances are lost, and focus is directed towards "us vs. them" narratives within echo chambers, it becomes easy to dehumanize and resent those outside your perceived group. Differences are amplified, and empathy is eroded by a lack of sustained attention needed to understand another's perspective.

The collective lack of sustained focus prevents meaningful dialogue, genuine understanding, and collaborative problem-solving. Society fragments into tribalistic groups, each trapped in their own filtered reality, unable to bridge gaps or find common ground.

Recognizing how your focus is being intentionally stolen is the critical first step in reclaiming your mental autonomy. This understanding illuminates why the conscious cultivation of Deep Focus is not just a personal benefit, but a vital act of resistance against the forces that seek to program and divide us. It is the beginning of reversing the ripple effect of subconscious programming and forging a new path toward collective awakening.

4. Understanding 4 D's for Creating Fear, Hate, and Division

We've established that Stolen Focus is not merely a personal inconvenience, but a deliberate and highly effective strategy. Its purpose is grander and more chilling than simple distraction; it is the fundamental lever used to systematically usher in fear, hate, and division. This process unfolds through a terrifying progression, a calculated descent through what I call the 4 D's, Distract, Disengage, Disarm, and Destroy. These are not separate, isolated tactics; they are intricately linked stages, each designed to pave the way for the next, eroding social cohesion and fracturing our shared reality.

Often interconnected and built upon each other in a reinforcing cycle, initial distraction can lead to a state of disengagement, making individuals more vulnerable to having their defenses disarmed. This can erode their independent thought and well-being, making them even more susceptible to future distractions and programming.

A. Distract:
Weakening Your Connection

Programming often starts by capturing and holding your attention, diverting it from what really matters. This is the initial, foundational step in the process. To distract means to overwhelm and fragment our attention with an incessant barrage of varied, often trivial, and highly sensational stimuli.

It's the constant notifications, the endless algorithmic feeds of social media, the hyper-edited entertainment, and the ceaseless flow of information that demands our attention every second of every day. Leveraging the very architecture of our digital lives, this phase exploits our biological wiring for novelty and immediate gratification. It ensures our Monkey Mind remains in perpetual, agitated motion, unable to settle on anything for long.

The goal of distraction is to prevent sustained focus. When your attention is constantly scattered, your mind is kept in a shallow processing state. You are prevented from engaging in critical thought, deep analysis, or thoughtful introspection. You become mentally fatigued, irritable, and highly susceptible to superficial messages. You remain trapped in your Subconscious Prison, constantly bumping against its walls, but too disoriented to ever see the full layout or the potential exit.

A distracted mind is easily manipulated. It lacks the capacity to discern nuance, making it simple to introduce fear-mongering headlines, sensationalized "us vs. them" narratives, and emotionally charged content that bypasses rational scrutiny.

B. Disengage:
Cultivating Apathy and Isolation

Once your attention is captured, programming aims to weaken your connections to critical thinking, empathy, and personal agency. Once focus is sufficiently distracted, the next stage is to disengage individuals from meaningful participation, collective action, and even genuine human connection.

This involves moving people from active, critical citizenship to passive consumption, fostering a sense of powerlessness, and encouraging isolation. Information overload, combined with the sheer exhaustion from constant distraction, can lead to a feeling of overwhelming helplessness. Why bother trying to understand complex issues when the information is endless and contradictory?

Echo chambers, fueled by algorithmic feeds, further reduce exposure to diverse viewpoints, diminishing empathy and the perceived value of real-world interaction. This stage erodes civic participation, reduces collective efficacy, and fosters a profound sense of individual apathy. People become less likely to engage in community, challenge authority, or believe in their ability to make a difference.

The "Subconscious Prison" becomes more comfortable, as venturing out seems futile or too exhausting. A disengaged populace is easier to control and divide. When people feel isolated and powerless, they become less likely to defend common values or challenge contentious narratives. Apathy allows fear to fester and hate to spread unchallenged. Without genuine engagement, communities fragment, and the bonds that hold society together weaken.

C. Disarm:
Stripping Away Critical Defenses

With your focus diverted and critical engagement weakened, programming seeks to dismantle your intellectual and emotional defenses. This is the most dangerous phase, designed to disarm individuals intellectually, emotionally, and socially. It strips them of their critical faculties, their emotional resilience, and their collective means of defense against manipulation and misinformation.

This involves a multi-pronged attack on trust and truth such as deliberately undermining faith in reliable institutions like mainstream media, scientific bodies, educational systems, and even government, flooding the information ecosystem with false narratives, propaganda, and conspiracy theories, making it almost impossible for a distracted and disengaged mind to discern what's real. Constant cycles of fear, outrage, and grievance are used to keep people in a heightened emotional state, making them less rational and more susceptible to impulsive, biased thinking.

By promoting simplistic solutions, emotional appeals over evidence, and tribal loyalty over rational inquiry, the very skills needed to challenge the narrative are degraded. Your internal "epistemic compass" is intentionally broken. A disarmed populace becomes profoundly vulnerable. They lose the ability to verify information, trust reliable sources, or collectively challenge powerful narratives.

They are left defenseless against manipulation, unable to identify the "thieves" operating in their minds or society. A disarmed mind is ripe for fear, easily convinced of existential threats. It becomes prone to hate, readily accepting demonizing narratives about "the other" when critical thinking is absent, and it fuels division, as people lose the capacity for empathy and reasoned debate, retreating into their own isolated, emotionally charged camps.

D. Destroy:
The Fragmentation of Shared Reality

The final stage can involve the erosion of your sense of self, values, and ability to think independently. This is the ultimate, grim outcome of the preceding stages. To destroy is to break down the fabric of shared reality, erode social cohesion, and dismantle the very foundations of trust and truth. It's the fragmentation of society into irreconcilable factions, perpetually locked in conflict. The cumulative effect of sustained distraction, widespread disengagement, and a thoroughly disarmed populace leads to a critical mass of individuals living in entirely different, often mutually exclusive, realities.

Civil discourse collapses, demonization becomes the norm, and the ability to find common ground or address real-world problems disappears. The result is societal breakdown, marked by chronic conflict, psychological distress, and the erosion of democratic principles. Trust evaporates, empathy becomes scarce, and the collective ability to cooperate for the common good diminishes. At this stage, fear, hate, and division are no longer just tactics; they are the dominant modes of social interaction, actively tearing communities, nations, and even families apart. The Subconscious Prison expands to become a societal prison, with humanity confined by its own inability to perceive truth or connect authentically.

Understanding these 4 D's is not about succumbing to cynicism; it's about recognizing the profound, systemic nature of programming that impacts not just individuals but entire societies. It illuminates why the journey to an Awakened Mindset, rebuilding your Knowledge Architecture by cultivating deep focus and mindful reset modalities, leveraging your Epistemic Principles, and dismantling your Mental Matrix, is not purely a personal quest, but a vital act of reclaiming our collective future and reversing this destructive ripple effect.

Chapter 5

The Power of Programming
The Unseen Architect: Mental Programming

Our thoughts, beliefs, and behaviors are constantly being shaped by forces we may not even realize. Mental Programming is the subtle and overt influence from media, technology, culture, societal pressures, and belief systems that mold our inner world.

1. The Fear Factor:
The Ultimate Lever of Control

As we have unveiled the 4 D's, Distract, Disengage, Disarm, and Destroy, as the deceptive progression that fragments our shared reality, we now directly confront their most potent output, The Fear Factor. This isn't about experiencing individual moments of fear; it's about an omnipresent, almost atmospheric condition of anxiety, apprehension, and insecurity that systematically influences perception, decision-making, and collective behavior. The Fear Factor represents a deliberate and widespread programming mechanism within the Mental Matrix, designed to keep individuals and societies in a perpetual state of heightened alert, susceptible to manipulation and control. It's the core emotion exploited by those who benefit from division, and the 4 D's are the tools used to amplify its reach and power. The 4 D's contribute directly to establishing and perpetuating the Fear Factor.

The constant stream of information and stimulation, the very essence of distraction, bombards your mind with endless, often conflicting, narratives of potential threats, whether they are health crises, economic downturns, political conflicts, or social anxieties. When your focus is perpetually scattered by this deluge, you lose the capacity for sustained, rational assessment. You cannot critically analyze the actual likelihood or severity of these threats. Instead, your subconscious, overwhelmed and unable to filter effectively, registers a constant hum of danger signals. This fragmented attention prevents you from discerning real threats from manufactured ones, making you vulnerable to exaggerated fears and easily triggered by sensational headlines or emotionally charged soundbites. Your mind becomes hyper-vigilant, scanning for threat without the capacity to process it thoughtfully.

Once Distraction leads to Disengagement, the Fear Factor escalates. When individuals feel disconnected from their communities, from collective action, and from a sense of shared purpose, they become isolated. An isolated individual feels inherently more vulnerable and less capable of facing perceived threats. The sense of "us vs. them" narratives, fueled by disengagement and echo chambers, fosters suspicion and distrust, often leading to fear of "the other." Without the collective strength of community or the shared wisdom of diverse perspectives, people feel more exposed and less resilient in the face of fearmongering. This isolation makes them more susceptible to narratives that promise security in exchange for conformity, or scapegoats to blame for their anxieties.

Disengagement leads the disarmament, stripping away the capacity for protection. The stage of Disarming is critical for the Fear Factor. When individuals are disarmed intellectually (lacking critical thinking skills), emotionally (lacking resilience), and socially (lacking trust in reliable information sources), they become defenseless against fear-based manipulation. The impact of constant fear is intellectual disarmament. If you can't discern truth from falsehood, or reliable sources from propaganda, every new piece of information becomes a potential trigger for anxiety. You cannot trust your own judgment, making you reliant on external narratives of fear. The constant emotional manipulation (e.g., outrage cycles, grievance politics) leaves individuals emotionally exhausted and fragile.

This emotional vulnerability makes them more susceptible to feelings of panic and despair when new fears are introduced. The breakdown of trust in institutions means there's no perceived reliable authority to turn to for reassurance or accurate guidance. This lack of shared understanding and reliable information amplifies uncertainty and fear.

The ultimate outcome of Destroy, the fracturing of shared reality and social cohesion, ensures that the Fear Factor becomes a dominant, self-perpetuating force. When society is fundamentally divided, when trust is annihilated, and when common ground is obliterated, a climate of perpetual anxiety emerges. Every interaction becomes a potential conflict, every difference a threat. The lack of collective capacity to address real problems (because we are too busy fighting each other) creates a constant background hum of existential dread. This fear then feeds back into the cycle, making people even more susceptible to distraction, disengagement, and further disarmament.

The Fear Factor, then, is not an accidental byproduct of modern life; it is a carefully curated state of being, deliberately amplified by the 4 D's. It operates within your Mental Matrix to keep you in a perpetual state of apprehension, ensuring you remain within the confines of your Subconscious Prison, unable to think clearly, connect deeply, or break free from the patterns that limit your true potential. Recognizing this manufactured fear is an essential step in reclaiming your power and stepping into an awakened state.

2. Hate Cycle:
The Weaponization of Division

We've investigated how the 4 D's, Distract, Disengage, Disarm, and Destroy systematically generate an inescapable Fear Factor, trapping individuals and societies in a state of chronic apprehension. Now, we confront the direct and devastating consequences often fueled by this fear, The Hate Cycle.

The Hate Cycle is not just a spontaneous outburst of anger; it is a self-perpetuating, programmed pattern of resentment, animosity, and often active dehumanization directed towards an "other" group or individual. It's a deeply destructive force within the Mental Matrix, carefully created to maintain division and control. Once activated, it feeds on itself, escalating conflict and fracturing the bonds of shared humanity. The 4 D's directly contribute to creating and spreading the Hate Cycle.

The relentless nature of distraction, by keeping our focus fragmented and shallow, makes it impossible to genuinely understand complex issues, diverse perspectives, or the underlying humanity of those we disagree with. The mind, constantly flitting, cannot engage in the sustained thought required for empathy. This fragmented attention is highly susceptible to simplistic "us vs. them" narratives.

When nuance is lost, and attention spans are fleeting, complex problems are reduced to easily digestible soundbites that often blame a specific group. This immediate categorization fosters an "in-group" mentality that thrives on identifying and demonizing an "out-group." The inability to focus on shared values or common ground means that difference is immediately perceived as a threat, a fertile breeding ground for animosity.

Once distraction leads to disengagement, the Hate Cycle intensifies. When individuals are disengaged from meaningful collective interaction, when echo chambers reinforce existing biases, and when genuine dialogue ceases, the opportunity for empathy and understanding with "the other" vanishes. Isolation and lack of genuine interaction with diverse groups make it incredibly easy to stereotype and dehumanize those outside one's immediate circle.

Without personal connection or a willingness to listen, "the other" becomes an abstract enemy, a convenient scapegoat for anxieties fueled by the Fear Factor. Disengagement reduces the likelihood of challenging hateful narratives because there's no personal stake or counterevidence provided by real human connection. The psychological distance created makes hatred easier to cultivate and maintain.

Breaking down truth and fueling resentment, this stage of disarming is crucial for cementing the Hate Cycle. When individuals are disarmed intellectually (unable to think critically) and socially (unable to trust reliable information), they become highly vulnerable to the spread of hate-filled propaganda and disinformation.

If critical thinking skills are eroded, individuals readily accept biased or false information that confirms their existing prejudices or fears about an "out-group." This allows hate to be justified with "facts" that are anything but true. The systematic undermining of trusted institutions (media, science) means there are no universally accepted sources of truth to challenge hateful claims.

People retreat into tribal sources of "information," where hate-filled narratives are amplified without critique. The constant bombardment of fear and outrage (leveraged by the Fear Factor) is easily channeled into hatred towards a designated target. Anger, frustration, and resentment find an easy outlet by blaming an "other." This emotional exhaustion also makes it harder to resist the pull of groupthink and collective animosity.

As a result, Destroy makes a prominent entry fracturing shared reality and societal cohesion, thus creating an environment where the Hate Cycle thrives and perpetuates itself. When society is fundamentally divided, when trust is annihilated, and when common ground is obliterated, hatred moves from individual feelings to systemic patterns of conflict. Different groups exist in their own fragmented realities, perceiving the "other" as an existential threat.

This leads to the demonization of entire populations, the breakdown of civil discourse, and an inability to find common solutions to shared problems. Hate itself becomes a destructive force, tearing apart families, communities, and nations. This self-sustaining cycle of animosity ensures that fear, hate, and division become the dominant mode of interaction, locking humanity deeper into the collective Subconscious Prison.

Understanding the Hate Cycle in conjunction with the 4 D's reveals the profound and destructive impact of systemic programming. It underscores why cultivating an Awakened Mindset, one rooted in Deep Focus, Epistemic Principles, and a reprogrammed Knowledge Architecture, is not merely about personal growth, but a critical act of compassion and collective liberation, vital for reversing this corrosive cycle and forging a path toward unity and understanding.

3. Victim Mentality:
The Abdication of Personal Power

We've illuminated how the 4 D's, Distract, Disengage, Disarm, and Destroy, orchestrate a ubiquitous Fear Factor, and ignite the destructive Hate Cycle. Now, to confront a profound consequence that traps countless individuals within their Subconscious Prison, the Victim Mentality.

Victim Mentality is not only a temporary feeling of being wronged; it's a deeply ingrained belief system within the Mental Matrix where an individual habitually perceives themselves as powerless, helpless, and perpetually suffering due to external forces beyond their control. It's a programmed state of being where life happens to them, rather than for or through them. This mindset erodes personal agency, fosters resentment, and keeps one from taking responsibility for their own path to freedom. The 4 D's systematically contribute to instituting and disseminating the Victim Mentality.

Distraction often hinders self-reflection and promotes external blame. The constant barrage of information and stimulation inherent in distraction keeps the mind perpetually outward-focused. It prevents the sustained attention and quiet introspection necessary for self-reflection, understanding one's own contributions to a situation, or identifying areas of personal agency.

When attention is constantly pulled externally, it becomes easier to externalize blame. Any challenge or discomfort is automatically perceived because of external forces (e.g., "The economy made me do it," "They made me feel this way," "I'm just unlucky"). This prevents the individual from recognizing their own capacity to influence their circumstances, solidifying the belief that they are a pawn in a game controlled by others. The Monkey Mind keeps attention on external "threats" rather than internal power. As Distraction leads to Disengagement, individuals become isolated, not just from collective action, but from their own sense of interconnectedness and support.

When communication channels are fractured, and genuine empathy erodes, individuals feel alone and utterly powerless to change their circumstances. Isolation reinforces the belief that one is on their own, unable to seek or receive help, and fundamentally incapable of standing up to perceived injustices. The lack of social connection and shared struggle makes personal setbacks feel overwhelming and insurmountable, deepening the conviction that they are helpless victims with no recourse. "Why bother trying?" becomes a default response, strengthening the passive stance of a victim.

Stripping away personal efficacy and resilience is a result of disarmament. The stage of disarming directly targets the very faculties needed to overcome a victim mindset. When individuals are disarmed intellectually (unable to critically analyze their own role or potential solutions) and emotionally (lacking resilience to cope with setbacks), they are left with a shattered sense of personal efficacy. Misinformation and propaganda often portray the world as chaotic and uncontrollable, or problems as too vast for any "one" person to influence.

This breaks down trust in one's own ability to make a difference, fostering learned helplessness. The constant emotional manipulation from fear and hate cycles leaves individuals emotionally drained and unable to cope with adversity. Every challenge feels like an insurmountable trauma, reinforcing the narrative of being perpetually victimized. When critical thinking is compromised, and the "epistemic compass" is broken, you cannot trust your own judgment or capacity to navigate life's challenges. This leads to the deep-seated belief that you are inherently incapable of taking effective action, thus, always remaining a victim.

In a world where everyone is a victim, caught in cycles of blame, powerlessness creates overall destruction. The ultimate outcome of Destroy, the fracturing of shared reality and widespread societal breakdown, creates an environment where the victim mentality becomes not just for individuals, but often for entire groups. In a society where trust is annihilated and common ground is lost; every group can easily perceive itself as the victim of another.

The inability to communicate or understand different perspectives leads to cycles of blame and grievance. Individuals, constantly exposed to narratives of being wronged or oppressed, find their personal victimhood reinforced by the perceived victimhood of their chosen group. This perpetuates a collective state of powerlessness, ensuring that fear, hate, and division become the dominant mode, preventing any move towards unity or solutions because everyone is busy pointing fingers rather than taking responsibility or finding their power.

The Victim Mentality, therefore, is not an inherent trait; it is a painstakingly constructed state of being, deliberately amplified by the 4 D's. It operates within your Mental Matrix to convince you that you are fundamentally powerless, keeping you firmly locked within your Subconscious Prison. Recognizing this sinister programming is the essential gateway to reclaiming your personal agency, understanding your true power, and beginning the profound journey of an Awakened Mindset.

4. The Algorithm Mind:
The External Architect of Your Prison

We've revealed how the 4 D's, Distract, Disengage, Disarm, and Destroy, orchestrate the Fear Factor and ignite the Hate Cycle contributing to the perpetual state of Victim Mentality. Now, to understand the deceptive force that leverages these 4 D's to shape not just individual minds, but collective consciousness, The Algorithm Mind. The Algorithm Mind refers to a human mind that has been unconsciously trained, conditioned, and increasingly controlled by the sophisticated digital algorithms that govern our online existence. These are the "if-then" rules that dictate what you see on social media, what news articles appear in your feed, what products are recommended, and even whose opinions you encounter.

It's a mind whose perceptions, thoughts, and behaviors are being subtly yet constantly nudged and shaped by external, profit-driven, or agenda-driven code, rather than by conscious, critical thought, or genuine, un-curated experience. Furthermore, it is a Mental Matrix that has been systematically optimized by external algorithms to serve their objectives, often at the expense of your own autonomy and well-being. The 4 D's systematically contribute to creating and solidifying the Algorithm Mind.

The Distraction inherent in our digital landscape is the primary tool algorithms use to hook our attention. Constant notifications, infinite scroll, short-form content, and gamified interactions are all scrupulously designed to fragment your focus and keep your Monkey Mind perpetually agitated and reactive. This constant bombardment and task-switching trains your brain for shallow processing and instant gratification, making sustained attention difficult. It creates a psychological dependency on external stimuli for engagement. Your mind learns to constantly seek the next "hit" of novelty or emotional response provided by the algorithm, rather than directing its own focus. This constant external pull prevents introspection and the development of internal clarity, making the mind highly susceptible to algorithmic direction.

Curating reality and isolation from divergent thought Disengages your perception. Once the mind is sufficiently distracted, algorithms proceed to Disengage you from a broad, unfiltered view of reality. They achieve this by creating sophisticated filter bubbles and echo chambers. By analyzing your past interactions, clicks, and preferences, algorithms curate a personalized feed that overwhelmingly confirms your existing beliefs and biases, while actively filtering out dissenting or challenging viewpoints.

This digital disengagement works to sever your connection to diverse perspectives and genuine dialogue. You become isolated within a self-reinforcing loop, where your beliefs are constantly validated by "like-minded" content. This profoundly limits your knowledge architecture, creating a narrow, biased worldview curated by the algorithm. The Algorithm Mind, in this stage, perceives its algorithmically generated reality as the only reality, cementing the "Subconscious Prison" with walls of comfortable, but limiting, information.

Undermining critical faculties and amplifying manipulative content Disarms your discernment. The process of Disarming is where the algorithm mind takes a firm hold. Algorithms are designed to prioritize "engagement," often meaning content that elicits strong emotional reactions (outrage, fear, excitement) or confirms existing biases. This systematic prioritization actively undermines your critical thinking skills and emotional resilience.

The constant exposure to sensationalized or emotionally charged content, without the intellectual space to critically evaluate it, dulls your discernment. Misinformation and disinformation, precisely because they often provoke strong reactions, are algorithmically amplified, leading the Algorithm Mind to accept falsehoods as truth. By constantly triggering fear and anger, algorithms leave the mind emotionally exhausted and highly susceptible to manipulation. An emotionally charged mind struggles to engage in rational thought, making it easier for algorithms to steer opinions and behaviors. As the mind becomes conditioned to receive its reality and emotional triggers from algorithms, its capacity for independent thought and self-directed action diminishes.

The Algorithm Mind loses its ability to question, to seek out contrasting views, or to trust its own internal compass. Fragmenting shared reality and fueling deep division destroys independent thought. The ultimate outcome of the Algorithm Mind, perpetuated by the 4 D's, is to destroy shared understanding and accelerate societal fragmentation. When billions of individual "Algorithm Minds" are each operating within their own distinct, algorithmically curated realities, the very foundation of common ground erodes.

The algorithmic reinforcement of fear, hate, and victimhood within these individualized echo chambers leads to deep irreconcilable divisions. The Algorithm Mind actively contributes to a world where rational discourse is replaced by tribal shouts, where empathy is replaced by suspicion, and where the "Subconscious Prison" expands to encompass entire segments of society, locked in perpetual conflict dictated by the unseen hands of code.

The Algorithm Mind, therefore, represents a new and profound layer of programming within your Mental Matrix, systematically installed and reinforced by external forces. It is the sophisticated driver behind the menacing Fear Factor, the relentless Hate Cycle, and the crippling Victim Mentality. Recognizing its influence is essential for reclaiming not just your personal autonomy, but for collectively forging an Awakened Mindset capable of transcending these manufactured divisions and reclaiming a shared, authentic reality.

5. Consumer Culture: The Endless Cycle of Desirous Programming

We've dissected how the 4 D's, Distract, Disengage, Disarm, and Destroy operate to create the Fear Factor to fuel the Hate Cycle, cementing Victim Mentality while amplified by the Algorithm Mind. Now, to confront the force that weaves through all these dynamics, dictating our sense of self-worth, happiness, and purpose, Consumer Culture. Consumer Culture is a societal system where the acquisition of goods and services is promoted as the primary pathway to identity, status, happiness, and problem-solving. It's a relentless narrative that tells us our worth is tied to what an individual owns, what an individual looks like, and what an individual consumes.

This culture actively programs our Mental Matrix with an insatiable desire for "more," perpetually pulling us away from internal contentment and authentic connection. The 4 D's systematically contributes to producing and propagating Consumer Culture. Keeping your focus on external acquisition is the utmost distraction. Consumer Culture perfectly utilizes the very essence of Distraction. Every advertisement, every social media trend, every new product launch is designed to capture and fragment your attention.

Your environment is saturated with calls to consume, from billboards to targeted ads on your phone. The constant bombardment keeps your focus perpetually outward, away from introspection, personal growth, or critical questioning of your true needs. Instead of looking inward for contentment or solving problems with ingenuity, your mind is trained to constantly seek the next external purchase as the solution to discomfort, boredom, or perceived lack. This endless stream of external stimuli prevents you from seeing through the illusion that happiness resides in acquisition, thereby maintaining the consumerist loop.

Disengagement often includes fostering isolation and material competition. Once Distraction has set in, Consumer Culture leverages Disengagement by undermining genuine human connection and fostering individualism. It promotes a competitive drive to "keep up with the Joneses," where personal worth becomes tied to visible markers of consumption rather than authentic relationships or community contribution. This leads to a disengagement from deeper societal issues and a focus on personal material accumulation. Instead of collective action or shared purpose, people become isolated in their pursuit of individual consumption, often experiencing envy and comparison. This isolation further entrenches the "Subconscious Prison," as individuals are less likely to question the consumerist narrative when they feel disconnected from alternative perspectives or communal support systems. The focus shifts from "us" to "me and my stuff."

Eroding self-worth and critical discernment is a major result of disarmament. The stage of Disarming is where Consumer Culture undermines personal power. It systematically erodes your innate sense of self-worth by constantly presenting ideals (body image, lifestyle, success) that are unattainable without endless consumption, thereby fostering a perpetual sense of inadequacy and lack. By linking happiness to products, Consumer Culture creates a cycle of unfulfilled desire and perpetual dissatisfaction. You are programmed to feel "not enough" unless you acquire the next new thing.

This constant feeling of inadequacy makes you emotionally vulnerable and susceptible to promises of external validation. It actively discourages critical thinking about the true cost of consumption, environmental, social, and psychological. It promotes superficiality and discourages questioning the deeper needs that consumerism purports to fill. Your Mental Matrix is disarmed of its capacity to discern authentic well-being from manufactured desire. Consumer Culture can lead to unsustainable debt and financial insecurity, trapping individuals in a cycle where they must constantly work to afford more, rather than pursue true freedom.

Undermining well-being and the destruction of social cohesion is the ultimate outcome of Destroy. The relentless pursuit of material accumulation, driven by the 4 D's, leads to environmental degradation, vast social inequality, and a spiritual emptiness that undermines true human flourishing. Unsustainable consumption patterns actively destroy the planet's resources, creating a literal crisis that generates immense fear and division. The constant focus on individual acquisition deepens the divide between "haves" and "have-nots," fostering resentment and hate based on material status. Community bonds weaken as competition replaces cooperation. Despite unprecedented material wealth in some parts of the world, widespread dissatisfaction, anxiety, and depression persist. This is because Consumer Culture actively destroys genuine sources of happiness, like deep connection, purpose, and inner peace, replacing them with fleeting external gratification. This perpetual state of unfulfillment further traps individuals within their "Subconscious Prison."

Consumer Culture, therefore, is not just an economic system; it is a precisely crafted, algorithmically driven program deeply embedded within your Mental Matrix by the 4 D's. It is a powerful force that sustains the Fear Factor by creating anxiety about not "fitting in, having enough, and/or living up to unattainable societal standards. Thus, influencing the Hate Cycle by being identified as the other, therefore, confirming Victim Mentality as a defense mechanism. Consequently, distracting us from our true nature and destroying our capacity for authentic connection and collective liberation. Acknowledging its menacing influence is a crucial step towards reclaiming your focus, challenging your programming, and stepping into a truly Awakened Mindset.

6. Performance Pressure:
The Relentless Grind of Conditional Worth

We've laid bare how the 4 D's are leveraged to create the Fear Factor, fueling the Hate Cycle, cementing Victim Mentality, harnessed by the Algorithm Mind, and driven into Consumer Culture. Now, to confront another powerful force that thrives within this environment, trapping countless individuals in a relentless cycle of striving and perceived inadequacy, Performance Pressure. Performance Pressure is the intense, often self-imposed, but profoundly externally influenced expectation to constantly achieve, excel, and meet ever-higher standards across all facets of life, from career and academics to social interactions, physical appearance, and even parenting. It's a deeply embedded program within the Mental Matrix that whispers, "Your worth is conditional. You are only valuable if you perform, achieve, and consistently prove yourself." This mindset robs individuals of intrinsic motivation, peace, and the ability to simply be without striving. The 4 D's systematically contributes to designing and achieving Performance Pressure.

Keeping focus on external validation and metrics distract us from true value. The constant Distraction inherent in our hyperconnected world bombards us with images and narratives of "success" and "perfection." Social media feeds display highlight reels of others' achievements, fostering comparison. The relentless pursuit of external metrics (likes, promotions, grades, physical appearance goals) demands our attention away from inner fulfillment or genuine connection. This fragmented attention prevents critical self-reflection on what really matters. Instead of defining success on your own terms, your focus is maliciously pulled towards external benchmarks and validation. You are perpetually distracted by the next goal, the next accolade, or the next external measure of worth, rather than finding peace in the present or valuing your inherent being. The Monkey Mind becomes fixated on the endless to-do list and the fear of falling short.

As Distraction leads to Disengagement, Performance Pressure intensifies by promoting fierce individualism and competition. The intense focus on personal achievement often leads to a reluctance to show vulnerability, ask for help, or genuinely collaborate, fearing that any perceived weakness will jeopardize one's standing. This disengagement from authentic relationships and collaborative support systems leaves individuals feeling isolated in their struggle. The pressure to maintain a façade of perfection prevents sharing burdens or seeking true connection. People become disengaged from their authentic selves, as their identity becomes conflated with their output. This deepens the "Subconscious Prison," as the fear of being "exposed" as less than reinforces the need to keep striving, even when exhausted.

Disarmament is implemented by eroding intrinsic worth and fear of failure. The stage of Disarming is where Performance Pressure critically impacts your inner resources. It systematically erodes your innate sense of self-worth, making it conditional on external achievements. It fosters an imminent fear of failure and promotes perfectionism as the only acceptable standard. The constant pursuit of perfection and the fear of falling short lead to chronic stress, anxiety, and burnout.

Every setback becomes a devastating blow to self-esteem, making individuals emotionally fragile and less resilient. This disarms joy and spontaneous creativity. Performance Pressure often stifles genuine curiosity and deep learning, replacing it with a focus on memorization and regurgitation for the sake of grades or metrics. It undermines intrinsic motivation, where learning is pursued for its own sake, replacing it with an external drive for validation. Your Mental Matrix becomes programmed to prioritize output over well-being and efficiency over genuine understanding. When your worth is tied to performance, any perceived imperfection or moment of rest triggers guilt and self-criticism, disarming your capacity for self-compassion and acceptance.

Destruction is formed as burnout, mental health crises, and societal unforgiveness. The ultimate outcome of Destroy is tragically evident in the societal consequences of unrelenting Performance Pressure. It breaks down individual well-being and fosters a highly competitive, unforgiving societal climate. Relentless striving without genuine fulfillment leads to widespread burnout, severe mental health crises (anxiety, depression, imposter syndrome), and a profound loss of meaning. Relationships suffer under the strain, and overall life satisfaction dwindles, despite apparent "success." A culture driven by Performance Pressure becomes ruthlessly competitive, often sacrificing collaboration and empathy for individual gain. This fuels a climate of judgment and unforgiveness, where perceived "failures" are harshly criticized, contributing to the broader cycles of fear, hate, and division. It destroys the fabric of a supportive community, replacing it with a hierarchy based on superficial achievement.

Performance Pressure, therefore, is not a benign force; it is a rigorously designed aspect of your Mental Matrix, deeply reinforced by the 4 D's. It traps individuals in an exhausting cycle of striving and perceived inadequacy, perpetuating the Fear Factor, intensifying the Hate Cycle (through competition and judgment), and exacerbating the Victim Mentality (when one inevitably "fails" to meet impossible standards). Identifying its deceptive influence is a crucial step towards reclaiming your inherent worth, redefining success on your own terms, and liberating yourself from this relentless grind in your journey to an Awakened Mindset.

7. Cultural Programming: The Invisible Blueprint of Your Reality

Finally, we arrive at the deepest and most pervasive "something before" that underpins all of these, Cultural Programming. Cultural Programming is the implicit and explicit process by which the dominant norms, values, beliefs, behaviors, traditions, and collective narratives of a society are transmitted across generations. It's the invisible operating system running in the background of your Mental Matrix, shaping your individual and group identity, defining what is considered "normal," "right," "wrong," "desirable," or even "real." From the language you speak to your moral code, your social customs, and your understanding of history, much of your core framework for navigating the world is culturally programmed, often without conscious awareness. The 4 D's systematically contributes to cultivating and preserving Cultural Programming, particularly in ways that lead to fear, hate, and division.

Cultural Programming distracts your perception by keeping you within the Cultural Narrative. Cultural norms themselves can become a form of Distraction. The constant demands of fitting in, adhering to social expectations, and engaging in culturally prescribed rituals or entertainment can divert attention from critical examination of the culture itself. Modern manifestations, such as the digital overload endemic to many cultures, are direct tools of this distraction. This perpetual outward focus prevents deep self-reflection on the origins or implications of your own cultural beliefs. You become too busy participating in the cultural flow to question its currents or challenge its underlying assumptions. It maintains the Monkey Mind, keeping attention on the surface-level demands and entertainment provided by the culture, rather than allowing a deeper inquiry into its ingrained programming. This ensures cultural programming remains invisible and unquestioned.

Disengagement enforces conformity and limits inter-cultural empathy. Cultural Programming can lead to Disengagement by fostering strong in-group/out-group mentalities. It often implicitly or explicitly discourages deep interaction with "outsider" cultures, ideas, or individuals who deviate from the norm. This disengagement fosters tribalism, where loyalty to one's own cultural group takes precedence over broader human connection.

When genuine inter-cultural dialogue is limited or discouraged, empathy across cultural divides becomes difficult. This perpetuates a sense of "us vs. them," where "the other" is often stereotyped, misunderstood, or even demonized. Individuals may disengage from global or universal humanitarian concerns, prioritizing their cultural group's interests, above all else, which solidifies the walls of the "Subconscious Prison" with cultural identity.

Disarmed by limiting worldviews and undermining critical thought about Culture. The stage of Disarming is where Cultural Programming profoundly impacts your cognitive and emotional defenses. It limits the frameworks of thought available to you by promoting a specific worldview as the absolute "truth," often downplaying or omitting alternative perspectives, historical injustices, or the complexities of cultural evolution. Cultural narratives can censor ideas, discourage dissent, and punish questioning, thereby undermining critical thinking skills within the cultural context. This makes it difficult to challenge deeply ingrained cultural biases or historical narratives, leaving you intellectually disarmed against misinformation that reinforces cultural prejudices. Deviating from deeply ingrained cultural norms can trigger intense shame, guilt, or fear of ostracization.

This emotional pressure disarms your courage to think independently or express authentic beliefs that might conflict with the dominant cultural program. Your Mental Matrix is conditioned to conform, making individual challenge exceptionally difficult. It can disarm the universal moral compass by teaching that what is "right" or "wrong" is solely determined by your culture, leading to an inability to critically assess cultural practices or recognize universal human rights, thus easily fueling hatred and division. Perpetuating historical conflicts and social fragmentation creates division and destroys social cohesion.

The ultimate outcome of Destroy is profoundly evident in how rigid or divisive Cultural Programming can lead to perpetual conflict and social fragmentation. Especially when rooted in historical grievances, nationalistic fervor, religious dogma, or racial/

ethnic supremacy, it can actively destroy inter-cultural trust and cooperation. It perpetuates cycles of inherited fear and hate, turning "us vs. them" into entrenched, seemingly unresolvable conflicts. This fragmentation prevents global collaboration on shared challenges, leading to widespread suffering and the literal destruction of lives and resources. The "Subconscious Prison" becomes a global construct, where humanity is divided and locked in perpetual conflict by the very blueprints of its diverse cultural matrices.

Cultural Programming, therefore, is not just a descriptor; it is the deep, often unseen, layer of your Mental Matrix that has been systematically installed and reinforced by the 4 D's. It defines your perceived reality, perpetuates cycles of Fear, Hate, Victimhood, and Consumerism, and often binds you within a Subconscious Prison built by unquestioned traditions and beliefs. Understanding this foundational programming is crucial for discerning your authentic self from inherited narratives and beginning the profound journey of an Awakened Mindset.

Chapter 6

The Depths of Cultural Programming:
Your Inherited Mind's Construction

We've explored Cultural Programming as the foundational blueprint of your Mental Matrix, the pervasive "something before" that shapes your reality. But how, precisely, is this invisible architecture installed? It's not a singular event; rather, your mindset is meticulously programmed through a lifelong immersion in various societal faculties, institutions and systems, designed to transmit values, norms, and beliefs. Each faculty, with its unique set of influences and objectives, contributes layers of code to your internal operating system, often without your conscious awareness. These are the primary channels through which the dominant narratives and expectations of your culture are impressed upon your mind, directly influencing what you come to believe about yourself, others, and the world.

The family unit is your first and most influential programmers, shaping foundational beliefs about ***love, safety, worth,*** and ***the world*** through spoken words, unspoken expectations, and emotional dynamics.

The Educational System aids in programming through most of our very formative years. Beyond academic knowledge, schools transmit societal values, norms of conformity, competition, authority, and often, a specific worldview or historical narrative.

Media and information ecosystems foster programming in shaping your perception. From traditional news and entertainment to the constant flow of digital content and social platforms, these channels inundate your mind with narratives, ideals, fears, and biases, powerfully shaping your perception of reality and self.

Religious and spiritual institutions play major roles in programming certain beliefs. These faculties often provide comprehensive moral frameworks, cosmologies, community structures, and definitions of purpose or identity, deeply embedding specific belief systems.

Government and legal systems leave a programmed stamp on society. Through laws, policies, symbols, and national narratives, these systems define citizenship, rights, responsibilities, and the very structure of society, dictating how power is perceived and exercised. Economic structures program unrealistic value.

Systems like Consumer Culture actively program desires, values related to material acquisition, status, and success, fundamentally influencing your sense of worth and priorities. Social norm conformity due to societal expectation has been prevalent. From childhood friendships to adult professional networks, the desire to belong drives conformity to unspoken rules, trends, and collective expectations, powerfully shaping behavior and thought. Each of these facilities acts as a potent programmer, consistently installing the code that forms your programmed mindset and constructs the walls of your Subconscious Prison.

Understanding their individual and combined influence is crucial for identifying the origins of your beliefs and beginning the work of conscious reprogramming. Think of the culturally programmed mind as an inherited mind. While it's crucial to clarify that this inheritance is not genetic, it is inherited in the most profound and ubiquitous non-biological sense. As we just discussed, cultural programming involves the systematic transmission of norms, values, beliefs, behaviors, and narratives from one generation to the next, through all the "faculties" we mentioned (family, education, media, etc.).

These are "downloaded" into your Mental Matrix from birth, forming the foundational layers of how you perceive and interact with the world. You inherit a pre-existing cultural "operating system." You don't arrive on Earth and invent language, social customs, or moral frameworks from scratch. Instead, you assimilate the ones that are already in place, passed down from your ancestors and immediate community.

Much of this inheritance happens subconsciously, through observation, imitation, conditioning, and the very air you breathe within your cultural environment. It's often invisible, precisely because it's the default setting you received. So, while not genetic, the term "inherited mind" powerfully conveys the idea that this cultural programming is received from what came before you, profoundly shaping your internal world before you even have the conscious capacity to question it. It truly is the "something before" that defines so much who you believe you are and how you see the world.

1. General Belief Systems:
The Core of Your Inherited Mind

Establishing that your Cultural Mind is an inherited mind, a blueprint downloaded from the "something before," we now turn our attention to the specific faculties that perform this profound programming. These are the foundational structures through which society's norms, values, and narratives are transmitted, deeply embedding themselves within your Mental Matrix. The most fundamental of these programmers, Belief Systems. Belief Systems encompass the deeply held convictions, tenets, and worldviews that define reality for an individual or a group. These aren't just thoughts; they are the very lenses through which you interpret information, make decisions, and form your identity.

Whether religious, philosophical, moral, or ideological, belief systems provide frameworks for understanding purpose, right and wrong, and humanity's place in the universe. They shape your values, dictate what you perceive as truth, and influence your emotional responses to the world around you. This makes them incredibly potent programmers of your Subconscious Prison, often operating invisibly as unquestioned truths that dictate your perceptions and actions. Fundamental beliefs and deeply ingrained assumptions about yourself, others, and the world that are often unconscious and taken for granted.

Early life experiences and significant events and interactions shape core beliefs about safety, trust, and worthiness. Cultural Norms and societal expectations are broad, often unspoken, beliefs about how things are and how people should behave influencing our perceptions of the way things “should” be based on ingrained cultural and societal beliefs. Repeated patterns and associations that create automatic responses and beliefs are learned from past experiences and conditioning. As a result, holding onto familiar beliefs, even if limiting, due to discomfort with uncertainty, manifests fear of the unknown or change.

This foundational conditioning acts as an invisible boundary, defining the limits of what we consider "possible" or "safe." For example, a child raised in a household where worthiness was tied strictly to academic achievement or obedience grows into an adult who feels a deep, subconscious anxiety whenever they stop "producing" for the system. Similarly, cultural norms regarding the "traditional" life path, graduate, work, consume, retire, create a powerful psychological anchor. Meanwhile, any deviation from this script is perceived by the nervous system not as freedom, but as a threat to survival. We choose the "familiar hell" over the "unfamiliar heaven" because the *subconscious* prioritizes the certainty of the prison over the unpredictability of the open field. This is why we stay in soul-crushing jobs or toxic dynamics.

Consequently, the Matrix has programmed many of us to believe that the discomfort of change is more dangerous than the slow decay of the status quo. To break this cycle, we must recognize that our "fear of the unknown" is actually a manufactured response designed to keep us from discovering that the unknown is where our true power resides.

2. Programming Through Subconscious Influences:

The Unseen Architects of Your Reality

While explicit belief systems lay a significant foundation for your inherited mind, much of your Mental Matrix is constructed by forces far more imperceptible and ubiquitous. These are the subconscious influences, the environmental cues, non-verbal messages, habitual patterns, and underlying emotional currents that program your mindset without ever reaching your conscious awareness. These influences operate in the background, shaping your perceptions, reactions, and automatic behaviors. They are the implicit biases, the unstated rules, and the deeply ingrained emotional responses absorbed from your surroundings, long before you could critically evaluate them.

This form of programming is exceptionally potent because it bypasses your conscious guard, quietly installing code directly into the deepest layers of your inherited mind, further solidifying the walls of your Subconscious Prison with invisible mortar. Unconscious absorption of beliefs, values, and emotional patterns from caregivers and the environment, indistinct cues in media or advertising that can bypass conscious awareness and influence thoughts and behaviors, unconscious attitudes and stereotypes that affect our understanding, actions, and decisions, and unconscious links between certain stimuli and emotional responses formed through past experiences can programmed you without your conscious awareness. Additionally, hypnotic suggestions such as messages received in a state of heightened suggestibility can influence subconscious beliefs, behaviors, and perceptions.

3. Programming Through the Power of Habit:

The Automation of Your Reality

While much of your Mental Matrix is shaped by subconscious influences operating beneath your awareness, the true entrenchment of this programming occurs through repetition. This brings us to the profound and often underestimated force of Habit. Programming through the Power of Habit reveals how repeated actions, thoughts, and emotional responses, whether consciously chosen or subconsciously initiated, forge deep neural pathways in your brain.

These pathways automate behavior, creating efficient routines that bypass conscious decision-making. What begins as a single action, repeated consistently over time, becomes a powerful program running on autopilot. This automation, while seemingly efficient, fundamentally reinforces the existing code within your inherited mind, making your programmed responses and perceptions feel immutable.

The power of habit transforms your Subconscious Prison from a theoretical construct into a lived reality, with its walls fortified by every unexamined routine. Behaviors and actions performed regularly become automatic and ingrained, shaping daily routines and overall lifestyle. Meanwhile, repeated ways of thinking about situations can become habitual, limiting flexibility and creativity. Moreover, repeated associations between certain triggers and emotional responses can create automatic emotional reactions and emotional conditioning promoting the acceptance of established social habits, norms, and expectations without conscious thought.

Crucially, sticking to these familiar habits and comforts, even when they are no longer beneficial or actively detrimental, acts as a formidable barrier of resistance. This isn't about laziness; it's rooted in a deeply ingrained fear of the unknown and a profound discomfort with change. The subconscious mind, wired for safety and predictability, perceives deviation from established routines, no matter how unfulfilling, as a threat. This powerful resistance ensures that the doors of your Subconscious Prison remain firmly shut, prioritizing the illusion of security over the discomfort of growth and the promise of liberation.

4. Programming Through Religion:
The Habitual Architect of Faith and Morality

We've examined how the Power of Habit relentlessly automates our reality, solidifying patterns and beliefs into the very fabric of our Mental Matrix. This automatic reinforcement, often rooted in a fear of the unknown, extends far beyond simple daily routines. For billions, it forms the bedrock of their spiritual and moral landscape, transforming profound belief systems into deeply ingrained practices from the earliest moments of life.

Consider the rhythmic Sunday services, the nightly prayers, the seasonal rituals, or the consistent communal gatherings, for many, these are not merely conscious choices but deeply etched habits. From birth, we are often immersed in these practices, absorbing their rhythms and messages long before conscious understanding takes root. Going to places of worship, participating in ceremonies, or observing sacred traditions becomes a powerful, often unquestioned habit, solidifying the beliefs and narratives within our inherited mind.

Programming through Religion represents a profound and often inescapable layer of cultural programming. It instills comprehensive moral frameworks, cosmologies that define the universe and humanity's place within it, and powerful narratives of purpose, belonging, and identity. Through sacred texts, communal rituals, authoritative figures, and the promise of ultimate meaning or salvation, religious programming directly shapes your deepest convictions, ethical codes, and understanding of reality. It's a fundamental architect of your Subconscious Prison, defining not just what you believe, but how you are allowed to believe, often with absolute certainty by establishing beliefs and rules that are often presented as absolute truths, limiting questioning and independent thought.

Repetitive actions that can reinforce specific beliefs and create emotional connections to the religious framework along with social pressures influence conformity to religious beliefs and behaviors within a community. Meanwhile, these prescribed rules for behavior shape one's understanding of right and wrong. Using fear of divine punishment and hope as a promise of a reward to encourage adherence to religious teachings, religious leaders and texts often hold significant authority, influencing belief without personal critical evaluation.

Chapter 7

Societal Programming: The Labyrinth of Social Engineering and Civic Indoctrination

1. Programming Through Ideologies: The Political and Social Architects of Reality

Religion is unique because it simultaneously inhabits the internal world of belief (Culture) and the external world of structure (Society). It functions as a "Universal Operating System" that synchronizes the individual's identity with the collective's organization. By discovering how deeply ingrained Belief Systems, especially those formed through the consistent practice and immersion of Religion, program your inherited mind, we now turn to another potent force that shapes your Mental Matrix, Ideologies.

While religion often provides a cosmic and moral framework, Ideologies are systems of ideas and ideals that offer explanations for how the world is and, crucially, how it should be. These are the political, economic, social, and philosophical blueprints that define societal problems, propose solutions, and dictate who has power and why.

From capitalism to socialism, nationalism to globalism, individualism to collectivism, ideologies provide ready-made lenses through which you interpret events, align with groups, and understand your place in the collective. Just like religious programming, ideologies are not only intellectual constructs; they are powerfully assimilated, often from birth, through education, media, family narratives, and peer influence. They install robust programs into your Subconscious Prison, shaping your values, dictating your loyalties, and governing your perceptions of justice, fairness, and truth. These ingrained ideological frameworks define your "in-group" and "out-group," influencing your allegiances and biases, often without conscious examination.

Ideologies program foundational beliefs that shape our understanding of how society should function (political, economic, social). Selective storytelling and information dissemination promote a particular viewpoint and demonize opposing, creating a strong sense of belonging for adherents while fostering suspicion or hostility towards those outside the ideology. Using fear, anger, and/or hope to bypass rational thought and encourage unwavering loyalty to the ideology encourages reliance on charismatic leaders or influential figures to dictate the "correct" way of thinking. In return, consuming information primarily from sources that align with the ideology, reinforce existing beliefs and limit exposure to diverse perspectives.

2. Programming Through Language:
The Unseen Architect of Your Perception

While Ideologies provide structured blueprints for understanding the world, these powerful mental models are not abstract constructs floating in the ether. They are precisely built, transmitted, and solidified within your Mental Matrix through the very air you breathe and the words you hear. Language is far more than just a tool for communication; it is a fundamental programmer of your perception, thought, and ultimately, your reality. The words we use, the phrases we habitually employ, and the grammatical structures of our native tongue subtly but profoundly shape how we categorize information, understand concepts, and even process emotions.

It frames what we can conceive as possible and what remains outside our cognitive boundaries. More powerfully still, Language is the vehicle of narratives and storytelling. From the personal anecdotes we tell ourselves, to the myths that define cultures, and the political narratives that shape nations, stories create emotional resonance and embed beliefs far more effectively than mere facts. These narratives, woven with specific Language, frame how you perceive events, define who is "us" and who is "them," and instruct you on what to value, fear, or desire.

Through this constant linguistic immersion, your Subconscious Prison is fortified, with Language serving as the invisible bars that define the very limits of your thought and perception. The way information is presented (positively or negatively) can significantly influence perception and belief. Using emotionally charged words to sway opinions and create biases, shaping understanding and perception through comparisons, internal dialogue that reinforces beliefs and impacts self-esteem and behavior, and constructing and reinforcing specific worldviews and values are all forms of how we become programmed through Language.

3. Indoctrinated Education System:
The Formal Architect of Your Inherited Reality

While Language shapes the very boundaries of your perception and frames your understanding of the world, this linguistic programming finds a deliberate and structured amplification within a powerful societal faculty, the Education System. From your earliest years, the education system has acted as a primary, formal architect of your Mental Matrix. It is designed not just to impart knowledge and skills, but to systematically transmit culturally sanctioned norms, values, historical narratives, and models of behavior. Through curriculum design, classroom dynamics, and the implicit messages conveyed by its structure, the education system thoroughly programs your inherited mind.

Crucially, Language is the bedrock of this educational programming. It dictates how concepts are presented, how history is framed, what stories are prioritized, and how "truth" is defined. The specific terminology, narratives, and communication styles embedded in lessons directly influence your understanding of the world, your place within society, and even the very way you are taught to think and express yourself. This structured linguistic immersion deeply engraves programs into your Subconscious Prison, shaping your worldview and defining the parameters of acceptable thought and success within the cultural paradigm.

The Education System systematically installs its programming through various explicit and implicit mechanisms, deeply shaping the Mental Matrix and reinforcing the Subconscious Prison. The specific subjects, facts, and theories chosen for instruction (e.g., historical narratives, scientific models, literary canons) directly inform what is considered "truth" and "important" within the culture. Equally powerful is what is not taught, alternative perspectives, marginalized histories, or critical analyses, which implicitly defines what is unimportant, irrelevant, or even taboo.

Emphasis on memorization over analytical thought can program obedience and discourage questioning of established facts or authority. Grading systems, rankings, and individual achievement focus can program a mindset of scarcity, comparison, and the need to outperform others, reinforcing aspects of Performance Pressure.

Learning to sit still, follow instructions, adhere to schedules, and operate within strict hierarchies' programs discipline, obedience, and adaptation to institutional structures. Students learn implicit lessons about social hierarchies, gender roles, power dynamics, and societal expectations through teacher-student interactions, peer dynamics, and school culture, even if these are not explicitly taught. The consistent experience of adult authority figures (teachers, administrators) and the expectation of compliance trains individuals to respect and obey hierarchical structures. Additionally, programming a focus on measurable outcomes and conformity to specific knowledge sets, often de-emphasizing creativity, diverse thinking, or holistic development.

Grades, awards, and disciplinary actions condition behavior, programming individuals to seek external validation and avoid perceived failure. The system precisely channels individuals towards specific paths (e.g., academic vs. vocational) and instills values preparing them for their perceived roles within the economic and social structures of the culture. School environments facilitate intense peer socialization, where acceptance often depends on conforming to group norms and values, further reinforcing cultural programming. Through these interwoven mechanisms, the education system acts as a powerful factory of the programmed mindset, systematically building the conceptual walls that define individual and collective reality, making it incredibly difficult to see beyond the prescribed curriculum of life.

4. Programming Through the Healthcare System: The Authority Over Body and Being

We've investigated how the Education System acts as a formal architect, using Language and structured curriculum to program your Mental Matrix. But this deliberate shaping of your inherited mind doesn't operate in isolation. In a striking example of interwoven societal control, the programming initiated by education is often profoundly reinforced and expanded by another powerful faculty, the Healthcare System.

Consider, the deeply ingrained, often unspoken, mandate that underpins your entry into formal learning: "Can't go to school without your shots." This seemingly simple requirement immediately establishes a fundamental layer of programming. From a very young age, you are taught that your bodily autonomy, your health, and even your participation in society, are contingent upon adherence to external directives issued by medical authority. It's a foundational lesson in compliance and trust in the system's prescribed solutions.

Programming through the Healthcare System extends far beyond mere medical treatment. It actively shapes your beliefs about your body, illness, healing, and the very nature of well-being. Through its models of disease, the role of medical experts, the emphasis on pharmaceutical solutions, and the very Language used to discuss health, it instills a specific worldview.

This system programs your Subconscious Prison with narratives of vulnerability, dependence on external authority for wellness, and often, a disengagement from your own innate healing wisdom. It dictates not just how you react to illness, but how you perceive health itself, solidifying your reliance on its established protocols and perpetuating a specific, often passive, relationship with your own physical and mental well-being. While often focusing on identifying and treating illness rather than promoting holistic well-being and prevention, it places significant trust in doctors and medical institutions, potentially leading to passive acceptance of diagnoses and treatments.

Additionally, the pharmaceutical Industry influence the marketing and promotion of medication as primary solutions for various health issues. Nevertheless, fear of illness and mortality through constant reminders of potential health risks can create anxiety and dependence on the healthcare system. Sometimes focusing on specific symptoms or body parts rather than considering the interconnectedness of mind, body, and spirit.

5. Programming Through Economic Systems:
The Architects of Desire and Worth

We've surveyed how various societal influences, from family and education to media, religion, education, and healthcare systematically program your Mental Matrix, shaping your beliefs, values, and perceptions. Now, we turn to a force that profoundly orchestrates much of our daily striving and defines our sense of worth in the material world, Economic Systems.

Programming through Economic Systems refers to the ways that the structures, values, and demands of a society's economic model (such as capitalism, consumerism, and labor markets) instill specific beliefs about success, value, scarcity, and human purpose. These systems don't just facilitate transactions; they actively dictate what is considered valuable, how that value is acquired, and even how individuals perceive their own worth in relation to material accumulation and societal contribution.

Through constant messaging, the structure of work, the pursuit of financial security, and the prevalent culture of consumption, economic systems become incredibly potent programmers of your Subconscious Prison. They establish the "rules of the game" for survival and thriving, profoundly influencing your aspirations, anxieties, and the very definition of a "good life," often binding you to cycles of external striving and a sense of perpetual lack.

6. Historical Narratives Programming:
The Architects of Collective Memory and Identity

We've just examined how Economic Systems program your Mental Matrix, dictating desires, shaping your perception of worth, and defining the very "rules" of societal engagement. Yet these economic realities are rarely presented in a vacuum; they are profoundly legitimized, explained, and emotionally charged by the stories we tell ourselves about the past. This brings us to a powerful and often unexamined source of programming, Historical Narratives.

Programming through Historical Narratives refers to the deliberate and unconscious ways that the stories of the past, who the heroes and villains were, what events are glorified or omitted, and what "lessons" are drawn, shape our collective memory, identity, and understanding of the present. These aren't just factual accounts; they are carefully constructed frameworks that imbue meaning into our existence, justify current societal structures (including economic ones), and prescribe future possibilities.

Through textbooks, monuments, media portrayals, national holidays, and familial lore, these narratives are deeply embedded into your Subconscious Prison. They tell you who "we" are, what "we" have overcome, who "they" are, and why certain power structures, ideologies, or economic systems are "natural," "just," or "inevitable." This programming of the past dictates our perception of the present, influencing our loyalties, our fears, and our willingness to either perpetuate or challenge the established order.

7. Programming Through Scientific and Technological Paradigms:

The Architects of Accepted Reality

We've uncovered how Historical Narratives craft our understanding of the past, shaping collective identity and legitimizing present structures. Often intertwined with these historical accounts is a powerful narrative of human progress, driven by breakthroughs in knowledge and innovation. This leads us to another potent and often unquestioned source of programming, Scientific and Technological Paradigms.

Programming through Scientific and Technological Paradigms refers to the ways that the dominant scientific understandings, accepted methodologies, and the very tools and applications of technology shape our perception of what is real, what is true, and what constitutes a valid solution to a problem. These paradigms are not just about facts; they establish the boundaries of rational thought, define what is "provable," and dictate how we approach understanding the world around us.

Through education, media, industry, and the ubiquitous presence of technology in our daily lives, these paradigms instill a specific worldview into your Mental Matrix. They program your Subconscious Prison by defining authority (e.g., "scientific consensus"), prioritizing certain types of knowledge (e.g., empirical, quantifiable), and influencing our trust in experts and technological solutions over intuitive wisdom or alternative approaches. This programming dictates not only how we solve problems but also how we perceive problems in the first place, often binding us to solutions presented by the very systems that benefit from these paradigms.

Chapter 8

Programming Through Trauma:

The Architect of Survival Responses and Fragmented Self

We've learned how Scientific and Technological Paradigms shape our understanding of the external world, defining what is considered logical, verifiable, and solvable. Yet, beneath the veneer of rationality and technological advancement lies a raw, deeply personal, and often unacknowledged form of programming that fundamentally distorts our inner reality and survival mechanisms, Trauma.

Programming through Trauma refers to the profound and often unconscious ways that deeply distressing or overwhelming experiences bypass normal cognitive processing, instantly imprinting powerful survival programs into the very core of our Mental Matrix. Unlike other forms of programming that build up over time through repetition or social conditioning, trauma can fundamentally alter your perception of ***safety, trust, and self-worth*** in a single, devastating moment.

When a traumatic event occurs, the mind and body are wired to survive. This survival response, while essential in the moment, creates deeply ingrained patterns, beliefs, emotional triggers, and behavioral reactions, that continue to operate on autopilot long after the threat has passed. This direct, visceral programming fortifies the walls of your Subconscious Prison not with ideas, but with fear-driven responses, protective mechanisms, and often a fragmented sense of self. It dictates how you react to perceived threats, influences your relationships, and can hold you captive in cycles of fear, anxiety, or avoidance, often without conscious awareness of its root cause.

1. Generational Curses Programming Through Generational Trauma:

The Echoes of Unresolved Pain

We've revealed how Trauma can, in an instant, bypass conscious thought and imprint powerful survival programs directly into your Mental Matrix, fragmenting your sense of self and dictating your responses to perceived threats. Yet the deep and often invisible wounds of trauma are not always confined to the individual who directly experienced them. They can, with chilling regularity, reverberate and program across generations, becoming an enduring legacy of unresolved pain.

This leads us to Generational Trauma, also known as intergenerational or transgenerational trauma. This concept refers to the profound psychological, emotional, and even biological effects of trauma that are transmitted from one generation to the next, impacting individuals who did not directly experience the original traumatic event. It's the silent carrying of burdens, fears, and coping mechanisms from ancestors, deeply embedding them into the fabric of succeeding generations.

Generational Trauma is a powerful form of inherited programming that subtly but profoundly shapes the Mental Matrix of entire family lines and communities. It stems from severe, overwhelming events (such as war, genocide, slavery, systemic oppression, displacement, chronic abuse, or widespread poverty) that overwhelmed the coping capacities of previous generations. The effects of this unresolved trauma manifest in descendants through learned behaviors and coping mechanisms. Children unconsciously absorb the maladaptive coping strategies of their traumatized caregivers, such as hypervigilance, emotional numbing, distrust, avoidance, or aggression. These become ingrained behavioral patterns.

Descendants may inherit distorted core beliefs about safety, trust, the world's benevolence, and their own self-worth, even without knowing the specific traumatic event that originated these beliefs. For instance, a generalized sense of dread or a constant need for external security can be passed down. Difficulty managing emotions like anxiety, depression, anger, or shame can become a family pattern, stemming from ancestors who lacked the capacity or safety to process their own trauma. Scientific studies are increasingly suggesting that trauma can leave biological imprints by altering how genes are expressed (epigenetic modifications), potentially influencing stress responses and emotional regulation in future generations. This indicates a physiological component to the inherited programming. Trauma can be passed through family stories and/or the purposeful silence around stories, traditions, worldviews, and narratives that reinforce the enduring impact of the original trauma.

Generational Trauma fortifies the Subconscious Prison with unseen walls built from the past. It dictates responses, creates anxieties, and influences relationships, often causing individuals to live out patterns of fear, scarcity, or self-sabotage that originated long before their birth. Recognizing this form of programming is a crucial step towards breaking these cycles and reclaiming a future free from inherited suffering.

2. The Silent Generation (1928-1945): Programmed by Scarcity and Sacrifice

As we've just explored the concept of Generational Trauma, how the profound wounds of the past can subtly but powerfully program succeeding generations, we now turn our attention to the first specific cohort through which we can observe this phenomenon in action, The Silent Generation. Born during the Great Depression and coming of age during World War II, this generation was not just shaped by history; they were deeply programmed by an environment of scarcity, sacrifice, and the urgent demand for conformity and resilience.

Programming the Silent Generation was an intense process driven by unprecedented global crises. Their formative years instilled a unique set of beliefs, values, and behaviors that prioritized stability, duty, and quiet adherence to societal norms above individual expression or dissent. This programming laid a bedrock for many of the cultural tenets that were later transmitted, both directly and indirectly, to subsequent generations, contributing to the very fabric of our Subconscious Prison. Rooted in the Great Depression, the scarcity mindset was created as result of limited resources creating the core belief that since resources were limited that waste was a sin and the idea that "saving for a rainy day" was paramount.

The behavioral imprint of this generation was frugality, resourcefulness, avoidance of debt, preference for stability over risk, and a deep-seated anxiety about financial security. This directly programmed a scarcity mindset into their Mental Matrix. Rooted in WWII, duty and sacrifice created the idea that suffering is inevitable, therefore, influencing the core belief that individual needs are secondary to the collective good (nation, family, community) and that hardship is to be endured without complaint. This generation has strong work ethic, patriotism, civic engagement, a willingness to sacrifice personal desires, emotional stoicism "suck it up", and a profound sense of obligation. This programming fostered a deep commitment to Performance Pressure based on duty.

Societal and military influence on this generation resulted in conformity and obedience which created the core belief that social order, adherence to rules, and respect for authority were essential for stability and safety; standing out or dissenting can be dangerous. This influenced a behavioral imprint of compliance, traditionalism, a preference for stability, aversion to challenging the status quo, and a strong value placed on modesty and humility. This reinforced the "if you have nothing nice to say..." and the "Imperfection Trap" programming.

As a response to trauma, this generation practiced emotional stoicism and resilience surrounded by the core belief that emotions, especially negative ones, should be contained; visible struggle is a weakness. This created a behavioral imprint for this generation characterized by a tendency to internalize pain, minimize emotional expression, avoid discussions of personal struggle, and maintain a calm exterior even amidst inner turmoil. This is a direct manifestation of Programming through Trauma, where emotional processing was suppressed for survival and stability.

The Silent Generation was the generation that influenced trust in Institutions, creating the core belief that the government, established media, and traditional institutions are largely trustworthy and act for the common good. Moreover, leaving a behavioral imprint of high civic participation (voting), reliance on mainstream news, acceptance of established social structures.

The Silent Generation's programming created individuals who valued hard work, stability, quiet perseverance, and fitting in. These traits, while crucial for rebuilding a post-war world, also inadvertently laid the groundwork for certain elements of the Subconscious Prison, such as the suppression of authentic self-expression, an ingrained fear of scarcity, and a deep-seated compliance that was then passed down through indirect means to their children and grandchildren. This generation's trauma responses became the silent, often invisible, directives for those who followed.

3. The Boomer Generation (1946-1964): Programmed by Post-War Abundance and Shifting Authority

Following the Silent Generation, forged in scarcity and sacrifice emerged the Boomer Generation. Born in the aftermath of World War II's victory and during an unprecedented economic boom, this cohort was programmed by a dramatically different set of circumstances, post-war abundance, rapidly expanding opportunities, a burgeoning consumer culture, and a complex relationship with authority, both adherence to, and ultimately, rebellion against. Programming the Boomer Generation was a multifaceted process. While they inherited some of the Silent Generation's values, their formative years presented new paradigms that profoundly shaped their Mental Matrix, contributing to a unique set of programs that would profoundly influence global society and future generations.

Post-War Boom influenced an optimism and abundance mindset with the core belief that the world is expanding, opportunities are limitless, and progress is inevitable; hard work guarantees upward mobility. This influenced a behavioral imprint characterized by a sense of optimism, belief in progress, willingness to consume, and a drive for material accumulation. This directly programmed an abundance mindset, in contrast to the Silent Generation's scarcity, within the emerging Consumer Culture. Early childhood conformity was present in this generation. Adherence to traditional values, family structures, and societal norms (often passed down from the Silent Generation) remained as core beliefs.

However, rebellion during adolescence and young adult hood influenced a different set of core beliefs that included questioning of established authority, social norms, and traditional institutions (e.g., Vietnam War protests, Civil Rights movement, counterculture). This created an internal conflict and a new form of anti-establishment identity, creating a behavioral imprint of widespread conformity (e.g., suburbanization, traditional family structures), followed by significant social activism, challenging of authority, and pushing for individual freedoms.

The emergence of youth culture influenced emphasis on self-expression with core beliefs that encouraged personal expression, individuality, and questioning traditional values are important. In return, this created a behavioral imprint of the development of distinct youth cultures (music, fashion), advocacy for civil rights, gender equality (second-wave feminism), and environmental awareness. This marked a shift away from the enforced conformity of the Silent Generation. The rise of television during this time influenced media saturation, created the core belief that information and entertainment are easily accessible, furthermore, leaving a behavioral imprint that television was the best source for information, allowing television to ideally influence their worldview, consumer desires, and perception of major events (e.g., televised war, news cycles). This amplified Programming through Media.

Another core belief of the boomer generation is that success is earned through individual effort and competition; education is the pathway to opportunity. Therefore, creating a behavioral imprint characterized by strong drive for professional achievement, a focus on climbing corporate ladders, and valuing educational credentials. This reinforced Performance Pressure with new avenues for expression.

The Boomer Generation's programming reflected a complex interplay of inherited values, external prosperity, and revolutionary social shifts. They were programmed to be agents of change in some respects, yet simultaneously deeply shaped by the emerging forces of consumerism and media. Their influence created distinct patterns of wealth accumulation, individualism, and a redefinition of societal roles, profoundly impacting the Subconscious Prison and setting new conditions for the generations that followed.

4. Generation X (1965-1980):
Programmed by
Disillusionment and Self-Reliance

Having evaluated the Boomer Generation's experience of post-war abundance and their complex relationship with authority, we now shift to Generation X. Born into a rapidly changing world, this cohort was programmed by a unique blend of disillusionment with institutional promises, a rise in familial instability, and an early immersion in evolving technology. Often labeled the "latchkey generation," their formative experiences instilled a deep sense of self-reliance, skepticism, and adaptability, fundamentally shaping their Mental Matrix.

Programming Generation X was less about overt ideological drives and more about adapting to a landscape where traditional societal structures seemed less dependable. Their experiences often led to an internalized program of "if you want something done right, do it yourself," contributing unique walls to their Subconscious Prison that set them apart from their predecessors. Rooted in social shifts, familial instability and the "Latchkey Kid" Phenomenon created the core belief that authority figures (parents, institutions) may not always be present or reliable; one must largely fend for oneself. Thus, creating a behavioral imprint of extreme independence, resourcefulness, self-sufficiency, a preference for autonomy, and often an emotional stoicism or a tendency to internalize problems due to early self-management. This experience reinforced aspects of the "Imperfection Trap" and the suppression of emotional needs, as external support was often absent.

The boomers' idealism and events influenced skepticism and cynicism creating the core belief that Institutions, politicians, and grand narratives, like the American Dream, are often untrustworthy; promises are likely to be broken. Therefore, creating a behavioral imprint with a pragmatic, often jaded outlook, a questioning of authority, a strong desire for authenticity and transparency, and resistance to being "marketed to." This programming directly countered the optimism of the Boomers and fostered a heightened awareness of societal hypocrisy, impacting their relationship with Programming Through Media.

Bridging analog and digital, technological adaptability influence that technology is a tool for convenience, efficiency, and self-directed information-gathering. This was the first generation to grow up with cable television (MTV's influence was profound), personal computers, and the early internet. They became tech-savvy adapters, comfortable with new tools but less dependent on them than later generations. This allowed for new avenues of Programming Through Media, but also tools for individual exploration.

Work-life balance and pragmatism were the core beliefs of this generation as a reaction to Boomer Workaholism. Work is a means to an end; personal life and fulfillment are paramount; efficiency in work is valued over excessive hours. A strong work ethic when engaged, but a clear boundary between professional and personal life. They value flexibility and often seek meaningful work over just climbing a ladder, redefining elements of Performance Pressure. Often overlooked or underestimated between larger, more vocal generations (Boomers and Millennials). Generation X leads a quiet resilience, a preference for working independently, and sometimes a reluctance to self-promote further contributing to Suppressed Self-Expression and a less noticeable need for external validation compared to some cohorts.

The Generation X's programming produced a cohort known for its resilience, adaptability, and independent spirit. While these traits often served them well in navigating a turbulent world, the underlying programming also solidified aspects of the Subconscious Prison around trust, emotional expression, and the often-solitary burden of self-reliance, which they, in turn, transmitted to the generations they raised.

5. The Millennial Generation (1981-1996):
Programmed by Digital Connectivity and a World of High Expectations

Having discovered Generation X's programming by disillusionment and self-reliance, we now turn to the Millennial Generation. Born at the cusp of the digital revolution, Millennials entered a world defined by unprecedented technological connectivity, a post-9/11 global landscape, and an intense environment of expectation, often inherited from their Boomer and Gen X parents. Programming the Millennial Generation has been a complex process, marked by constant digital immersion, economic volatility, and a unique emphasis on purpose and social validation.

This generation's Mental Matrix is highly influenced by instantaneous information, social comparison, and pervaded sense of having to "do it all," leading to new and reinforced walls within the Subconscious Prison. Rooted in technology and media, the digital native immersion, created the core belief that information is always available; connection is constant; personal identity is often curated online, influencing innate comfort with the internet, social media, and mobile technology. This created an "always-on" mentality, fostering new forms of Distraction and Performance Pressure through constant comparison with curated online lives. This amplified programming through media and Information Ecosystems exponentially.

Inherited from Boomers/Gen X, high expectations and achievement pressure influenced the core belief that you must achieve success, have a college degree, and find a meaningful career; participation trophies meant everyone's a winner. With a strong drive to succeed, often accompanied by significant academic and career pressures. This programming contributed to a heightened sense of Performance Pressure and an underlying anxiety about not meeting perceived standards, even in the face of economic challenges. Post-9/11, recessions created economic instability and debt burden for this generation influencing the core belief that economic security is elusive, traditional pathways to success are not guaranteed, and debt is a normal part of life.

Experience of the dotcom bust, 9/11, and the 2008 financial crisis during formative career years, creating massive student loan debt, difficulty entering stable job markets, and a lingering sense of financial insecurity. This reinforced elements of a Scarcity Mindset despite the abundance narrative and bred distrust in economic systems.

Influenced by Gen X and new awareness, social consciousness and purpose became the forefront of this generation creating core beliefs that include, but not limited to, social justice, diversity, inclusion, and making a positive impact are vital; personal values should align with work. High engagement in social causes, desire for meaningful work, emphasis on corporate social responsibility. While positive, this could also lead to new forms of Performance Pressure (the pressure to be "good enough" socially) and Guilt Programming if not actively engaged in activism.

As results of previous generation parenting styles of "suck it up" and "figure it out" complex influenced *Helicopter Parenting* and *Structured Childhood* creating the core belief that children need constant supervision, guidance, and protection; participation is more important than winning. Often grew up in more structured environments than Gen X, with less unsupervised time. This could lead to a preference for clear instructions, a reliance on external guidance, and sometimes a struggle with independent problem-solving when faced with ambiguity, directly affecting their Epistemic Compass. The *"Chosen"* or *"Special"* Generation, millennials have been faced with the core belief they could do anything, however, leading to a clash with the harsh economic realities they faced. Moreover, creating a potential for disillusionment when reality doesn't match expectations, sometimes fostering a Victim Mentality when confronted with unexpected hardships.

The Millennial Generation's programming has created a cohort that is highly adaptable to technology, socially aware, and driven by purpose, but also often burdened by economic anxiety, comparison culture, and the weight of unfulfilled expectations. Their unique position, bridging the analog past and the digital future, has generated distinct walls within the Subconscious Prison, impacting their sense of worth, their relationship with authority, and their pursuit of authentic peace.

6. Generation Z (1997-2012):
Programmed by Hyper-Connectivity, Global Crises, and Authentic Imperfection

Following the Millennials, a generation navigating high expectations and digital immersion, we arrive at Generation Z. This cohort is the first to be born into a world where the internet, smartphones, and social media have always existed. They are true "digital natives," coming of age amidst a relentless flow of information, global crises, and a complex relationship with both curated online identities and a longing for genuine authenticity.

Programming Generation Z is a profound and often contradictory process, marked by constant digital saturation, heightened awareness of systemic issues, and an acute sensitivity to mental well-being. Their Mental Matrix is wired for instantaneous information and global interconnectedness, leading to unique and often intense walls within their Subconscious Prison, impacting their sense of security, self-worth, and their relationship with reality.

True Digital Natives with ubiquitous digital Immersion created the core belief that the world is instantly accessible; identity is fluid and can be expressed (and curated) online, and immediate answers are the norm. Therefore, creating a behavioral imprint that is characterized by an innate comfort with technology, constant multi-platform engagement, and rapid information processing. This leads to new forms of Distraction and an expectation of immediacy. The very concept of "reality" is often blended with the digital, impacting their Epistemic Compass.

Social media and comparison culture created intense Performance Pressure and anxiety for Generation Z influencing core beliefs that self-worth can be tied to online validation; everyone else's life appears curated and perfect. High rates of social media use for entertainment, connection, and identity expression. However, this comes with significant reported increases in anxiety, depression, sleep loss, and phone addiction. The constant "compare and despair" cycle fuels intense Performance Pressure and a heightened sense of the “Imperfection Trap” if their reality doesn't match the idealized online world.

Global awareness and social justice activism has created existential anxiety and purpose-driven action internalized by the core belief that systemic issues (climate change, racial injustice, economic inequality) are urgent and demand action, influencing highly socially conscious and politically active individuals. This fosters a strong desire for purpose and authenticity but also contributes to eco-anxiety and a sense of overwhelm from global problems inherited from previous generations. While witnessing economic crises, Generation Z, core belief is that economic stability is uncertain and traditional pathways are risky; debt is a heavy burden. More financially conservative than Millennials, greater interest in saving, investing (including cryptocurrencies), and exploring entrepreneurial or "gig economy" avenues.

This stems from witnessing the Great Recession and other economic challenges during their formative years, reinforcing elements of a Scarcity Mindset. Mental health is a legitimate concern and should be openly discussed. Self-care is essential for this generation, creating greater willingness to talk about mental health struggles and seek support. Paradoxically, they report higher rates of anxiety and depression, suggesting that while awareness is high, the underlying programmed pressures and digital stressors are intensely impactful. This highlights a struggle with the "Suck It Up" programming, attempting to break it.

Authenticity is paramount; personal expression and individuality are valued, while labels are often rejected. This creates a desire for genuine connection and a critical eye toward anything perceived as inauthentic. This is a potential counterprogram to the curated "Performance Pressure" of social media but also presents its own challenges in finding unprogrammed self-expression.

The Generation Z's programming creates a cohort that is highly connected, socially aware, and purpose-driven, yet often burdened by unique forms of digital anxiety, the weight of global crises, and the constant navigation of curated versus authentic reality. Their unique position makes them potential pioneers in dismantling elements of the Subconscious Prison, but also highly susceptible to its evolving, digitally infused walls.

7. Generation Alpha (2010-2025):
Programmed by Immersive Digital Reality and Inherited Global Crises

Building on our understanding of the Generation Z, digital immersion and anxiety, we now turn to Generation Alpha, the current, youngest generation. Born entirely within the 21st century, often to Millennial parents, this cohort is defined by an unprecedented level of technological immersion, the influence of Artificial Intelligence, and a foundational awareness of global crises that have shaped their entire young lives.

Programming Generation Alpha is a process unlike any before, happening within a blended reality where digital and physical worlds are seamlessly integrated. Their Mental Matrix is being wired for immediate access, personalized experiences, and constant global awareness, establishing entirely new forms of walls within their Subconscious Prison and reshaping their understanding of learning, social connection, and even personal identity.

Ubiquitous integration, hyper-digital and AI natives, generation Alphas believe that technology and AI are intrinsic, personalized tools for every aspect of life, learning, entertainment, connection, and problem-solving. They have never known a world without smartphones, tablets, streaming services, and AI voice assistants (Siri, Alexa). This cultivates an expectation of instant gratification, intuitive interfaces, and adaptive systems. This is the ultimate evolution of Programming through Scientific and Technological Paradigms, and Media and Information Ecosystems, where digital tools are not just present, but fundamentally integrated into their daily cognitive processes and learning styles.

Blended reality and immersive experiences created the core belief that the lines between physical and digital spaces are fluid and learning and play often occur in virtual or augmented environments, influenced by early exposure to VR/AR, gamified learning, and online social platforms that create immersive experiences. This can blur the distinction between actual and simulated reality, potentially impacting their Epistemic Compass in discerning truth from sophisticated digital constructs.

Personal lives are often publicly documented from birth (by parents' social media use); online identity requires curation. Growing up with their milestones shared online creates an early awareness of public image and potential future digital reputation. This introduces new forms of Performance Pressure and Fear Factor related to online presentation and judgment, even at a young age.

In return, inherited Global Crises and high social consciousness beliefs regarding climate change, social justice issues, and economic instability are urgent realities that demand action enforcing the idea that collective responsibility is paramount. They are highly aware of global challenges from a noticeably young age (e.g., post-pandemic world, ongoing climate conversations). This fosters a strong drive for purpose, inclusivity, and sustainability, leading to early civic engagement but also a potential for profound eco-anxiety and the weight of inherited systemic problems. Personalized learning, education, and content consumption should be tailored to individual needs and preferences; therefore, content should be engaging and short form. For example, learning via AI-powered platforms and consuming bite-sized video content (e.g., TikTok, YouTube Shorts). This can lead to highly efficient knowledge acquisition in preferred formats but may also impact attention spans and the ability to engage with longer, less interactive forms of information or critical analysis.

For this generation, safety, emotional well-being, and structured development are paramount; children need support and guidance. Raised by Millennials who often prioritize structured activities and digital guardianship, lead to a preference for clear instructions and a potential reliance on external guidance, which contrasts with Gen X's "latchkey" independence. With Generation alpha, unlike many other generations, mental health is a valid concern, and open discussion and self-care are important. Growing up with increased dialogue about mental health, they are more willing to discuss their feelings. However, they are also experiencing rising rates of anxiety and depression, suggesting intense underlying programmed pressures and digital stressors. This continues the struggle with the "Suck It Up" programming, but from a younger, more vocal age.

Generation Alpha's programming is crafting a cohort that is hyper-connected, deeply global, and inherently adaptable to technological shifts. They are poised to lead breakthroughs in innovation and social impact, but their profound immersion in digital realities and the weight of inherited global crises will define the evolving walls of their Subconscious Prison, shaping their mental well-being, their perception of reality, and their path to authentic freedom.

Chapter 9

Programmed Perspectives:
The Invisible Lenses Shaping Your Reality

We've uncovered the vast "faculties" that construct your Mental Matrix, from the sweeping economic systems and historical narratives to the intimate details of family dynamics and generational imprints. Now, we turn our gaze inward, focusing on the very filters through which you perceive reality itself, Programmed Perspectives. Programmed Perspectives are the specific, often hidden, beliefs, assumptions, and interpretations that have been skillfully installed in your Subconscious Prison from the earliest moments of your life. These are not innate truths; however, they are lenses forged through a variety of means, from the seemingly innocuous rhymes of childhood to the potent narratives embedded in popular culture and the structured lessons of our formative years.

Consider the phrases you heard, the movies you watched, the games you played, each was a potent, often unnoticed, mechanism of programming. A simple affirmation can become a deeply ingrained lie, a cartoon character's journey can dictate a societal expectation, and playtime with a doll can predetermine a life's trajectory. These aren't just memories; they are the fundamental instructions that tell your mind what is "normal," what is "true," what is "expected," and how you "should" feel and react. This section will delve into these specific, everyday examples of Programmed Perspectives, revealing how these seemingly minor cultural touchstones and linguistic constructs exert immense power over your emotional responses, behavioral patterns, and ultimately, your ability to perceive your own authentic truth. By exposing these invisible lenses, we begin the profound work of consciously choosing a new way of seeing, and thus, a new way of being.

1. Sticks and Stones Programming: Words Do Hurt!

"Sticks and stones may break my bones, but words will never hurt me" is a profound lie, a programmed idea designed for compliance, and a direct offshoot of the "suck it up" mentality. This seemingly innocent rhyme, taught to children globally, is one of the most damaging pieces of linguistic programming embedded in our Mental Matrix. Words carry immense emotional charge. They can uplift, inspire, connect, but they can also wound, shame, demean, and traumatize. Psychological pain from words can be far more lasting and destructive than physical pain, which often heals more quickly.

Words shape our self-perception and identity. Being repeatedly called "stupid," "worthless," or "incapable" directly programs a person's core beliefs about themselves, impacting self-worth for decades. This phrase encourages the internalization of verbal abuse. Instead of processing the pain inflicted by words, the recipient is programmed to deny it, often turning the hurtful words into an inner critical voice. This phrase and life lesson carries a "suck it up" narrative and is a primary tool for teaching emotional suppression. It implicitly tells individuals that if they feel hurt by words, they are weak, oversensitive, or "wrong" for having that feeling. This forces them to disengage from their authentic emotional responses.

It teaches a fundamental denial of emotional reality. If you are told that words "can't" hurt, but you feel hurt, it creates a conflict between your inner experience and the programmed "truth." This can lead to confusion, self-blaming, and an inability to articulate your needs or boundaries. By dismissing the power of words, it inadvertently enables verbal abusers. If words don't "hurt," then the person using them isn't doing harm, and the victim has "no right" to complain. This program builds a strong wall within your Subconscious Prison around emotional vulnerability.

It prevents you from expressing your true feelings when verbally attacked, from setting healthy boundaries, and from seeking support for emotional wounds. It reinforces the Performance Pressure to be "tough" and unemotional and contributes to the Victim Mentality by teaching you to internalize and deny abuse rather than confronting it.

2. "If You Have Nothing Nice to Say, Don't Say Nothing At All": The Programming of Suppressed Truth

"If you have nothing nice to say, don't say nothing at all" was one of the most significant phrases of my life. I lived and still live by these very words, but I often wonder how many times I hurt myself not saying what I felt. Who was I really protecting? This phrase was not only used in Disney's Bambi, but it also became a pivotal phrase throughout history. On the surface, the intention of this phrase is noble, to prevent gratuitous meanness, bullying, and unnecessary cruelty. It aims to foster kindness and social harmony. And there's certainly a time and place for choosing tact and empathy over brutal honesty. However, the sinister deeper program embedded within this phrase teaches something far more damaging. This implicitly programs the idea that if a truth isn't "nice" or "positive," it's inherently hurtful and therefore should be withheld. This creates a false dichotomy where honesty, especially critical observation, or disagreement, is equated with aggression or negativity. This phrase elevates superficial pleasantness and social harmony above genuine expression. It teaches that one's authentic perceptions, thoughts, or feeling must be censored if they don't fit a "positive" or "nice" mold.

This forces a constant internal self-editing, contributing to a fragmented self that struggles to express its true nature.

By conditioning people to only speak "nice" things, it prescribes an environment where uncomfortable truths, necessary critiques, constructive feedback, or even simple factual observations that highlight imperfections are suppressed. This leads to unspoken resentments, unaddressed problems, and a collective inability to confront reality. If everyone adheres to this program, how can individuals receive honest feedback to grow? How can problematic behaviors or systemic flaws be addressed if no one is willing to speak about them for fear of being "not nice" or "negative"? This allows mediocrity and injustice to persist unchallenged. This phrase is a perfect complement to "suck it up." If "suck it up" tells you to endure emotional pain silently, "if you have nothing nice to say..." tells you to inflict the same silence on others when their authentic truth might cause discomfort. Both mechanisms promote a compliance with discomfort and an aversion to genuine emotional processing.

Thumper's observation about Bambi's wobbly legs was a simple, factual, and natural observation about a newborn's motor skills. There was no malice in it, only an accurate reflection of reality. By framing Thumper's comment as "picking on" or "mean," the narrative and the accompanying parental/educational reinforcement programs children to perceive any observation that highlights a perceived imperfection or difference as inherently hurtful or negative. This teaches a chilling lesson, "If you see something that deviates from an idealized 'perfect' image (like Bambi walking perfectly), and you don't fully understand it, the best thing is to keep silent.

Don't ask questions, don't voice your thoughts, don't state the obvious fact." This actively disarms curiosity, critical observation, and the very act of engaging with reality if it's not uniformly "nice" or "positive." Bambi resonated and influenced generations of humans with this subtle but incredibly powerful piece of programming. It's a foundational brick in the wall of the Subconscious Prison, teaching us to censor our authentic perceptions and protect a fragile, often fabricated, sense of "niceness" over genuine understanding and courageous truth-telling.

3. Programming Through Disney Movies: The Enchanted Architect of Idealized Reality

We've excavated how everyday phrases and activities install Programmed Perspectives; now we confront a cultural "steamroller" that shapes the very fabric of imagination and expectation from the earliest ages, Disney movies. These cinematic experiences are far more than mere entertainment; they are crafted narratives that act as powerful, enchanting facilities for programming belief systems, suppressing authentic self-expression, and limiting the perceived possibilities of reality for millions.

Programming through Disney Movies involves emotionally resonant installation of specific ideals, gender roles, societal expectations, and definitions of happiness and success. Through captivating animation, memorable songs, and archetypal characters, these films bypass rational defenses, embedding a potent, often unexamined, worldview directly into your Mental Matrix, particularly during highly impressionable childhood years. First, suppression of Authenticity through Idealization. Disney characters, especially princesses, often embody highly idealized forms of beauty, gentleness, obedience, or unwavering optimism.

Their journeys frequently culminate in external validation (a prince, a crown, acceptance). This programs children to believe that their worth is tied to fitting a specific, often physically and emotionally perfect, mold. It can foster the Imperfection Trap by creating a relentless comparison to an unattainable ideal, leading to the suppression of genuine feelings, "flaws," or unique personality traits that don't fit the "nice" or "pretty" persona.

Through various mechanisms Disney created belief systems about gender roles and relationships. Classic Disney narratives often feature passive female protagonists (like many early princesses) who are "locked up" or stuck in difficult circumstances, waiting patiently for a male rescuer. Happiness is frequently equated with finding a "Prince Charming" and achieving a "happily ever after" (often devoid of real-world complexities like financial stability, personal growth beyond marriage, or sustained partnership effort). This powerfully programs traditional, often limiting, gender roles (the damsel in distress for women; the heroic, problem-solving rescuer for men). It teaches that a woman's ultimate fulfillment and purpose lie in romantic love and domesticity, and that life's major problems are solved by an external, often masculine, figure.

These very mechanisms often limit perspectives on reality and power. Conflicts are often resolved through magical intervention, clear-cut good vs. evil battles, or the heroic actions of a single, often external, figure. The world is presented in stark binaries. This can program a simplistic view of complex problems, suggesting that real solutions come from external saviors or magical events rather than nuanced effort, internal work, or collective, collaborative problem-solving. It can disarm critical thinking, foster a reliance on external "heroes," and make real-world struggles seem daunting if they don't fit the neat narrative arc. The common ending of "happily ever after" implies a static, problem-free state once the "goal" (marriage and/or overcoming a villain) is achieved.

This programs an unrealistic expectation of life's trajectory, leading to potential disillusionment and a feeling of "failure" or "wrongness" when real life inevitably presents ongoing challenges and complexities. It reinforces the idea that true peace is an external achievement rather than an internal state developed through continuous effort. Disney movies, by virtue of their emotional resonance and early exposure, are incredibly potent architects of these Programmed Perspectives. They shape not just what children dream of, but how they dream, what they value, and who they believe they are supposed to become reinforcing the walls of the Subconscious Prison with enchanting, yet confining, narratives.

4. "Lining Up, Wait Your Turn, No Cutting": The Programming of Social Order

"Lining Up, Wait Your Turn, No Cutting" was one of the first things I was taught when I went to school ensuring we knew how to first "follow rules" and be compliant with authority. This is another classic example of behavioral programming designed for order and obedience, but with deeper implications. It teaches children to constantly defer to an external structure for movement, rather than relying on their own internal pacing or social negotiation. Being "in line" means minimizing individual expression or spontaneous movement. It's about becoming part of a uniform unit. Waiting your turn teaches patience, but it also teaches deference to a predetermined sequence and to those ahead of you in the hierarchy of the line.

The punishment for "getting out of line" strongly reinforces the negative consequences of non-conformity, teaching individuals to stay within prescribed boundaries. This instills a deeply ingrained program for social order, hierarchy, and adherence to rules that extend far beyond the classroom. It prepares individuals for accepting queues, bureaucratic processes, and social strata without questioning their fundamental purpose or alternative ways of organizing.

5. Fire Safety Drills:
Order, Obedience, and Emergency Compliance

While the obvious, benevolent intention is undeniably about physical safety and instilling vital skills for genuine emergencies, there's a powerful layer of implicit programming happening during constant fire drills in educational facilities in early years and workplace environments in later years. The drill teaches immediate, automatic, and unquestioning compliance to specific instructions given by an authority figure (teacher, principal, fire fighter). There is no room for debate, individual thought, or creative problem-solving in that moment, only synchronized action based on a pre-defined protocol.

Conformity under duress where everyone must follow the exact same path, in the exact same way, in the exact same order. This instills a deep-seated program that in times of perceived crisis or urgency, individual agency is suspended in favor of collective, compliant movement dictated by external rules. This prepares individuals for countless other scenarios in life where uniform behavior is expected under pressure, whether it's in a workplace, a government building, or even during a societal crisis where official directives must be followed without question. It reinforces the idea that order and obedience are paramount for collective safety.

6. D.A.R.E.'s Unintended Consequences:
Fueling Curiosity, Rebellion, and Economic Pathways

While the stated intention of the D.A.R.E. program was to inoculate children against drug use, its black-and-white messaging and didactic approach often created a Programmed Perspective that, for certain cohorts like Generation X and early Millennials, fostered outcomes precisely opposite to its goals such as heightened curiosity, a spirit of rebellion, and in economically challenged contexts, even an unwitting roadmap to illicit economic activity. The overall intention of this program was to educate on the dangers of drug use and deter use using scar tactics enforced by police officers.

The program comprehensively lists various drugs and displays it's varied packaging, showing what looks to be like the "substance". Describing their effects (even if framed negatively) and consistently highlighting the "taboo" nature of these substances, D.A.R.E. inadvertently demystified and, for some, even glamorized what was previously unknown. For naturally curious minds, the program's detailed warnings could transform into a "forbidden fruit" phenomenon. The constant focus on what not to do, paradoxically, made these substances more concrete and intriguing, especially for a generation already programmed with a degree of skepticism (Gen X) or a desire for new experiences (Millennials). Studies have indeed shown that early DARE curricula, in some cases, increased curiosity about drugs.

For adolescents, particularly those already programmed with a questioning of authority (like Gen X, who grew up with parents often perceived as absent or hypocritical, and institutions that sometimes failed), a direct, authoritative "just say no" message from a police officer could trigger a natural inclination towards defiance. This wasn't necessarily a desire to use drugs, but a psychological resistance to being told what to do by an external figure, especially if the message felt disconnected from their lived realities or if they observed adults around them using substances without negative consequences.

This taps into the inherent anti-establishment undercurrent in some youth. For children in economically challenged communities, DARE (and the broader "War on Drugs" narrative) inadvertently highlighted that there was a significant, albeit illicit, economy surrounding these substances. While emphasizing the dangers, the program also detailed the existence of drug use and distribution networks. In contexts where legitimate economic opportunities were scarce (a direct consequence of broader Economic Systems programming), and where other programming like Familial Instability (leading to lack of supervision) was prevalent, the drug trade could become a perceived pathway to income and status.

The program, in its attempt to warn, often exposed the nature of a lucrative black market without simultaneously offering viable, accessible alternatives for economic survival and aspiration. It painted a vivid picture of the "problem" but offered no corresponding solution to the underlying economic desperation that often drives individuals into such activities.

The tragic irony is that the generations most intensely subjected to DARE's original programming (Gen X and early Millennials) did indeed witness and participate in significant drug epidemics. This suggests that the program, in its monolithic and often fear-based approach, became another layer of Programmed Perspective that, rather than protecting, inadvertently contributed to the very issues it aimed to prevent, by misdirecting curiosity, triggering rebellion, and, for some, illuminating an otherwise unseen economic route within the already constructed walls of the Subconscious Prison.

Chapter 10

Programming Through Emotion:
The Affective Feedback Loop

1. Programming through Media:
Media as the Modern Propaganda Machine

When we view media through the lens of societal programming, the line between "content" and "propaganda" effectively disappears. In this context, Propaganda isn't just a government-issued poster; it is any curated flow of information designed to narrow the scope of thought and encourage a specific behavioral output.

Traditional Propaganda was often easy to spot because it was heavy-handed. Modern media programming is more effective because it offers the illusion of a wide spectrum of choice. Whether you are watching a sitcom, a news broadcast, or scrolling through a social feed, the underlying "programming" remains consistent as it reinforces consumerism, validates specific social hierarchies, and defines the boundaries of "acceptable" opinion. By providing a hundred different channels that all broadcast the same core values, the system ensures that the audience feels free while remaining boxed in.

From a psychological and sociological perspective, media acts as a secondary socialization agent that installs "cultural software", predefined sets of values, fears, and desires, into the observer's subconscious. This programming often operates on the "survival-mode" frequency of the ego, reinforcing a sense of lack, competition, and external dependency. By curating what is perceived as "normal" or "aspirational," media environments can effectively loop the human mind in a cycle of reactive consumption, where identity is derived from external validation rather than internal essence.

Consequently, Propaganda works by bypassing the logical brain and anchoring ideas in emotion, specifically fear, desire, and the need for belonging. Media programming uses these same triggers. By repeatedly associating certain behaviors with social "success" (desire) and others with "cancellation" or failure (fear), media programs the individual to police their own thoughts. Over time, these programmed responses feel like "common sense" or "objective truth," which is the ultimate goal of any propaganda campaign.

In the digital age, programming has become automated. Algorithms are designed to keep users engaged, which they achieve by feeding the individual more of what they already believe (confirmation bias). This creates "echo chambers" that function as personalized propaganda loops. These loops don't just reflect who we are; they actively program us to become more extreme versions of our current selves, making societal cohesion more difficult while making the individual easier to predict and control.

Ultimately, Programming through Media is the "soft power" equivalent of propaganda. It doesn't require force because it wins the battle for the mind by making the programmed values indistinguishable from the individual's own desires. Recognizing this is the first step toward "digital literacy", the ability to see the code behind the content.

2. External Validation and Attention-Seeking Behavior:
The Invisible Chains of Approval

One of the most devious and invasive programs we encounter is the deep-seated need for External Validation and Attention. What was once an occasional human impulse, in the modern era, morphed into a normalized, almost unconscious, daily drive. This behavior becomes "programmed" within us, from early childhood to the inescapable influence of digital platforms, and the profound impact it has on our individual well-being and the collective human experience. The Programming of External Validation and Attention-Seeking Behavior is a multi-layered process, woven into the fabric of our development and amplified by the very tools we use to connect.

The foundational programming begins in our earliest years. As infants and children, we are utterly dependent on caregivers for survival, love, and safety. Our brains are wired to seek connection and approval as a primary survival mechanism. Parental and caregiver approval becomes the forefront to our initial programming for approval. A child learns quickly that certain behaviors (e.g., sharing, being "good," achieving milestones) elicit positive responses (praise, smiles, affection, rewards), while others lead to disapproval or withdrawal. This creates a direct link, "My value and safety are tied to external approval". The nature of our early attachments can significantly influence this. Insecure attachment styles (anxious, avoidant) can foster a heightened need for external reassurance or a defensive detachment, both rooted in a fear of disapproval or abandonment. Children may internalize the belief that love and acceptance are conditional upon performance, leading to a lifelong pattern of seeking external achievements or recognition to feel worthy.

Beyond the family unit, broader societal structures continue the programming. Grades, awards, public recognition, and peer acceptance in schools reinforce the idea that external metrics define success and worth. Students learn to perform for the grade, the teacher's praise, or the admiration of classmates. Adolescence is a critical period where peer validation becomes paramount. Fitting in, being liked, and gaining social status often dictate behavior, fashion, and even opinions. The fear of social exclusion is a powerful motivator for conformity and attention-seeking within group norms. Before the digital age, television, magazines, and advertising presented idealized images of success, beauty, and happiness, implying that achieving these external benchmarks would lead to fulfillment and societal acceptance. Celebrity culture amplified the idea that attention equated to importance.

While the groundwork is laid early, social media platforms have acted as accelerators, transforming intermittent reinforcement into a constant “program" for External Validation and Attention-Seeking Behavior. Dopamine driven feedback loops provided by social media platforms are engineered using principles of operant conditioning. Likes, comments, shares, and follows become the main source of dopamine.

These are instant, quantifiable metrics that act as potent rewards. Each notification triggers the release of dopamine; the neurotransmitter associated with pleasure and motivation. The rewards are unpredictable. You don't know which post will "hit" or when. This variable ratio schedule is the most powerful for conditioning behavior, making users compulsively check and post, much like a gambler at a slot machine. Social media turns social acceptance into a visible score. Follower counts, likes, and view metrics become proxies for popularity, influence, and even self-worth. This creates an intense drive to constantly increase these numbers. Additionally, promoting curated identities and a performance culture. Users are incentivized to present an idealized, often unrealistic, version of themselves. Life becomes a performance for an unseen audience, where authenticity can be sacrificed for "likes."

This constant self-curation and performance reinforce the idea that one's value lies in how well one is perceived by others. Platform algorithms prioritize content that generates high engagement. This means content designed to provoke strong reactions, including attention-seeking or sensationalism, is often amplified, further rewarding and normalizing such behaviors. The ubiquity of smartphones ensures that validation is always just a tap away. This constant accessibility, coupled with the fear of missing out (FOMO), creates a continuous loop of checking, posting, and seeking external affirmation, making it an ingrained, almost unconscious, daily ritual. The business model of social media thrives on user engagement and attention. The more time users spend on platforms, the more advertising revenue is generated. This creates a powerful economic incentive for platforms to design features that encourage and perpetuate attention-seeking behaviors.

The normalization of External Validation and Attention-Seeking Behavior has far-reaching consequences, affecting individuals and the broader societal fabric. When self-worth is tethered to external approval, it becomes inherently unstable. A dip in likes, a critical comment, or a lack of attention can trigger feelings of inadequacy, anxiety, and even depression. This creates a perpetual state of seeking, rather than finding, internal peace. The pressure to perform for an audience can led to a disconnect from one's true self. Individuals may suppress genuine thoughts, feelings, or interests if they fear they won't be "liked" or validated. This can result in a superficial identity built on external perceptions rather than internal truth.

The constant pursuit of external validation, coupled with the inevitable comparisons to others' curated highlight reels, contributes significantly to heightened anxiety, social comparison stress, and feelings of loneliness and inadequacy. The dopamine loops created by social media can lead to behavioral addictions, where individuals feel compelled to constantly check their phones, post, and seek affirmation, disrupting sleep, focus, and real-world relationships.

Decisions may be unconsciously influenced by how they will be perceived by others, rather than what truly aligns with one's values or long-term well-being. Society becomes increasingly focused on outward appearances, curated lives, and superficial metrics of success. This fosters a universal comparison culture, leading to widespread dissatisfaction and a relentless pursuit of external benchmarks. Content designed to elicit strong reactions often thrives on social media. This can inadvertently reward extreme views and contribute to the formation of echo chambers, where individuals are primarily exposed to validating opinions, further entrenching divisions and reducing nuanced discourse. The programmed need for attention fuels influence marketing and consumerism. Individuals become unwitting conduits for commercial messages, blurring the lines between genuine connection and transactional relationships, and directing collective desires towards material acquisition.

When individuals and the collective are constantly engaged in the cycle of seeking and giving attention, it can divert focus and energy from critical self-reflection, meaningful community engagement, and addressing systemic societal challenges. The "program" keeps us busy performing, rather than deeply questioning. Erosion of trust can destroy genuine trust and authentic connection, leading to a sense of isolation despite hyper-connectivity.

Recognizing how deeply programmed the need for External Validation and Attention-Seeking Behavior has become is the first, crucial step towards awakening. It's not about blaming individuals but understanding the powerful forces that shape our behavior. By acknowledging these programs, we begin to create the necessary space to dismantle them, reclaim our inherent self-worth, and cultivate an internal compass that guides us towards genuine fulfillment, independent of the applause of the crowd. The path to an Awakened Mindset demands a conscious and sustained effort to reprogram our deepest behavioral patterns.

3. The Addictive Personality:
A Programmed Vulnerability

The idea of an Addictive Personality speaks to a vulnerability within the subconscious mind, a predisposition to seek external gratification, escape, or stimulation in compulsive, often self-destructive, ways. This isn't merely a random weakness; it is, in many profound ways, a programmed mindset. The Mental Matrix, layered with early childhood experiences, societal narratives, and the constraints of the Subconscious Prison, can inadvertently construct a fertile ground for addictive patterns to take root. When foundational needs for security, belonging, or authentic self-expression are unmet or distorted by programming, the mind, in its desperate attempt to find equilibrium or relief, can become wired to latch onto external sources, whether substances, behaviors, or even relationships, to fill an internal void. These are not inherent flaws, but rather deeply ingrained responses, often learned and reinforced, that make breaking free from the cycles of addiction a monumental, yet entirely possible, act of de-programming. The Addictive Personality can be seen as a complex tapestry woven from various threads of programming.

When individuals, especially during formative years, experience neglect, abuse, chronic stress, or lack of healthy emotional regulation models, their developing subconscious learns to associate certain external inputs with temporary relief or escape from pain. The "sticks and stones" lie, for instance, teaches emotional suppression, meaning pain is not processed but avoided. For example, a child growing up in a chaotic household where emotions are suppressed learns that numbing feelings with food, excessive screen time, or later, substances, provides a brief respite. This learned pattern of avoiding discomfort, rather than processing it, becomes a deeply ingrained program. The instant gratification offered by certain behaviors or substances then becomes a programmed "solution" to any form of internal distress.

Modern society is saturated with instant gratification. Social media "likes," video game achievements, fast food, and rapid-fire entertainment (like quick-cut cartoons or TikTok) provide immediate, powerful dopamine hits. The brain's reward pathways are designed to seek out and repeat behaviors that release dopamine. For example, a child constantly provided with digital devices or sugary treats to pacify them is being programmed to expect immediate rewards and to have a low tolerance for boredom or delayed gratification. This creates a neural pathway that constantly craves external stimulation. When older, the brain, programmed for these quick dopamine fixes, becomes highly susceptible to substances or behaviors that offer an even more potent and immediate "hit," making self-regulation incredibly difficult. This echoes the "lining up" programming, where external systems dictate gratification.

If the Mental Matrix contains deeply uncomfortable truths about oneself (e.g., the Imperfection Trap) or their perceived reality, the subconscious can program an escape route. Someone programmed with the Disney ideal of needing a "rescuer" or a "happily ever after" might find real life's complexities overwhelming. Instead of confronting these perceived failures or disempowering beliefs, they might escape into fantasy worlds (gaming addiction), compulsive spending (shopping addiction), or substance abuse, effectively trying to live within a self-created illusion that temporarily alleviates the pain of perceived reality. The addiction becomes a self-imposed, albeit destructive, "time loop" of avoidance.

Societal narratives, often propagated through advertising and consumer culture, equate happiness and success with constant acquisition, consumption, and heightened sensory experiences. If one is programmed to believe that a life of constant pleasure, like Phil Connors' early hedonistic phase in Groundhog Day, is the path to fulfillment, then the pursuit of that pleasure can escalate into an addictive pattern. The brain continually seeks novelty and intensity, pushing boundaries, leading to higher doses or more extreme behaviors to achieve the same initial "rush." This relentless pursuit of external "more" becomes the addiction itself.

Programming that suppresses individuality (e.g., "don't boast," conforming to rigid gender roles) can leave a deep void in an individual's sense of self and purpose. If a person's Authentic Self has been stifled by years of trying to fit a mold, they might seek to "find" themselves or "feel alive" through addictive behaviors. The temporary confidence from substance use, the community in a gaming clan, or the perceived "power" of risky behavior can become a substitute for a genuinely formed, self-validated identity, providing a false sense of belonging or purpose that then becomes incredibly hard to relinquish.

In essence, the Addictive Personality is often a highly sophisticated, albeit detrimental, coping mechanism that the subconscious mind develops in response to deeply ingrained programming and unmet needs, tragically trapping individuals in repetitive cycles until they consciously choose to de-program and reclaim their authentic power.

4. Desensitization: The Silent Programmer

In our quest to awaken, we must confront the subtle yet profound ways our minds are programmed to accept what was once unacceptable. Another sinister form of this programming is Desensitization. This psychological process diminishes our emotional, physiological, or critical responses to a stimulus after repeated exposure. Imagine the first time you witnessed a shocking image or heard a disturbing piece of news; your reaction was likely strong. Now, consider how often similar stimuli appears in your daily life.

Desensitization explains why that initial shock fades, why the disturbance becomes mundane, and how the abnormal can silently become the new normal. It is a powerful, often unconscious, form of programming that reshapes our perception of reality. Desensitization operates through a mechanism of gradual habituation, effectively rewiring our brains to reduce their reactivity to repeated inputs. This process, while sometimes used therapeutically (e.g., to overcome phobias), is often a passive and detrimental form of programming in the context of an unawakened mind.

The core mechanism of Desensitization is simple repeated exposure. When we are consistently exposed to a particular type of information, image, sound, or behavior, our nervous system and brain begin to adapt. Our brains are designed to be efficient; if a stimulus is constantly present and doesn't immediately signal danger or novelty, the brain gradually reduces its alert response. It learns to "filter out" what it perceives as redundant or non-threatening information. Consequently, what is frequently encountered becomes familiar, and what is familiar often begins to feel normal. This applies not just to neutral stimuli, but also to disturbing or morally questionable content, as the sheer volume and frequency of exposure wears down our initial resistance.

As repeated exposure continues, the emotional circuits in our brain that would typically fire in response to a stimulus begin to quiet down. This results in reduced emotional reactivity, meaning the shock, outrage, sadness, or fear that a particular event or image might initially trigger starts to lessen. We become less emotionally invested or affected. A critical consequence of Desensitization, particularly to suffering or violence, is a reduction in empathy.

When we are constantly exposed to images of pain, injustice, or tragedy without the opportunity to process or respond meaningfully, our capacity to genuinely feel for others can wane. The suffering of "the other" becomes less impactful and more abstract. A clear example of this is seen in news cycles: the first reports of a distant conflict might evoke strong sympathy, but as the conflict drags on and images of suffering become a daily fixture, many people find their emotional response dulling. They might still acknowledge the tragedy intellectually, but the visceral, empathetic connection diminishes.

Desensitization doesn't just affect our emotions; it subtly reprograms our cognitive understanding of what is acceptable or normal. As emotional responses lessen, the perceived severity or wrongness of a behavior or event can also decrease. What was once considered extreme or unacceptable might slowly shift towards being seen as "just the way things are," "unavoidable," or even "normal." Our minds seek consistency, so if we are repeatedly exposed to something that initially conflicts with our values, but we don't or can't act on that conflict, we may subconsciously adjust our internal frameworks to rationalize or accept the new reality. This can involve minimizing the harm, blaming the victims, or simply disengaging from critical thought.

This is where desensitization becomes a powerful programmer, as behaviors that were once considered rude, aggressive, superficial, or unethical can become normalized simply because they are seen everywhere. For instance, the prevalence of harsh comments, trolling, and public shaming online can desensitize individuals to the impact of their words, making online toxicity seem like a normal part of digital interaction. Similarly, the constant display of highly curated, often performative, lives on social media, or the dramatic conflicts on reality television, can desensitize us to the artificiality of these interactions, leading us to believe that such performative living is authentic or desirable.

Desensitization is not just an individual process; it spreads through social dynamics, creating a collective program. If a behavior or type of content becomes common within a social group; individuals may desensitize to it more quickly to fit in or avoid being seen as overly sensitive. Mass media, including news, entertainment, and social platforms, play a critical role in this collective programming. By repeatedly presenting certain narratives, images, or behaviors, media can collectively desensitize populations to issues, making them less likely to react or demand change. This can be seen in the normalization of certain political rhetoric, economic disparities, or even environmental degradation.

Consequently, the impact of Desensitization is profound and far-reaching. When we are desensitized, our internal alarm system is muted, making us less likely to feel the necessary moral outrage or urgency required to challenge injustice, advocate for change, or even recognize when our own boundaries are being crossed. A *Desensitized Mind* is also less likely to question what it sees or hears; the "shock value" that would normally trigger deeper inquiry is gone, leaving us more susceptible to manipulation and less able to discern truth from narratives.

Over time, what we are desensitized to can shift our personal and collective moral boundaries, allowing behaviors once considered unacceptable to slowly creep into the realm of the tolerable, or even the expected. Furthermore, if we are constantly exposed to problems but feel less emotionally impacted by them, we are more likely to become passive observers rather than active participants in creating a better world. The "program" encourages a state of complacent acceptance.

5. Music as the Program:
The Sonic Programmer

In our exploration of the Awakened Mindset, we uncover the imperceptible forces that shape our reality. Beyond the melody and deeply rooted in our subconscious, among the most prevalent, yet often overlooked, is music. Far from being mere entertainment, music is a potent, silent programmer, capable of influencing our emotions, thoughts, memories, and even our purchasing decisions. It bypasses our conscious filters, embedding messages and shaping our internal states in ways we rarely acknowledge. Understanding how music operates as a form of programming is essential to reclaiming our autonomy and consciously curating our inner landscape.

Music's power to program stems from its direct access to our emotional and subconscious processing centers bypassing the logical scrutiny we might apply to spoken words or visual information. Music has an unparalleled ability to evoke and transfer emotions, and this is its most immediate form of programming. Different musical elements, tempo, rhythm, melody, harmony, timbre, directly impact our physiological state. For instance, fast tempos can increase heart rate and arousal, while slow tempos can induce relaxation. Similarly, minor keys often evoke sadness or introspection, whereas major keys tend to create feelings of joy or triumph. Our bodies respond to these stimuli before our conscious minds can even process the sound.

Composers and producers are masters at manipulating these elements to create specific emotional experiences. A film score, for example, guides our feelings, telling us when to feel suspense, fear, or relief. Retail stores strategically use music to create a desired shopping mood, such as upbeat music for faster turnover or calming music for longer browsing. This isn't merely background noise; it's an intentional emotional program designed to influence behavior. Furthermore, we unconsciously mirror the emotional states conveyed by music. If a song expresses joy, our own internal state tends to shift towards joy. This "emotional contagion" is a powerful, non-verbal form of influencing our mood and energy without explicit instruction.

Music is deeply intertwined with memory, making it an incredibly effective tool for programming associations. A particular song can instantly transport us back to a specific time, place, or event, complete with the emotions we felt then. This is why advertising often uses nostalgic music to link products to positive past experiences; the music doesn't just remind us; it reactivates the entire emotional and contextual memory. Through repeated pairing, music can program associations between a specific melody or jingle and a product, brand, or even an ideology. Consider advertising jingles that stick in your head, or anthems associated with political movements, the music becomes an emotional shorthand for the message or product, often bypassing critical evaluation. Moreover, songs frequently tell stories or convey specific messages through lyrics.

When combined with powerful melodies and rhythms, these narratives can be deeply embedded in our minds, influencing our perspectives, values, and understanding of the world. Repeated listening further reinforces these programmed narratives. Repetition is a fundamental principle of programming, and music provides an ideal medium for it. The very design of popular music relies on repetition, through choruses, riffs, and hooks, to make songs memorable and "catchy." This constant repetition, even if consciously irritating, programs the melody and its associated lyrics or feelings into our long-term memory.

While blatant subliminal messages (ex. backmasking) are often debated and largely debunked in their direct effectiveness, music can exert subliminal influence in more subtle ways. The overall mood, the underlying lyrical themes, or even the cultural context of a genre can convey messages that are absorbed without conscious awareness. For example, music designed for relaxation can program a calm state, while aggressive music can program a heightened state of arousal or even aggression. In essence, music played in public spaces like stores, restaurants, and gyms acts as a constant, low-level program. It influences our pace, our mood, our perception of time, and guides our behavior (e.g., encouraging faster eating, longer browsing, or more intense workouts) without us ever consciously deciding to be influenced.

Beyond individual influence, music plays a powerful role in

programming collective identities and social norms. Music genres, artists, and anthems serve as powerful markers of group identity. Listening to certain music can program a sense of belonging, shared values, and collective emotion, reinforcing tribal affiliations and distinguishing "us" from "them." The themes, stories, and attitudes expressed in popular music can also reflect and reinforce prevailing cultural values, or, conversely, challenge them. Over time, repeated exposure to these musical narratives can program societal norms around relationships, success, rebellion, or consumerism. Historically, music has been faint background music in political broadcasts and can program emotional allegiance or dissent, bypassing rational argument.

The nature of Music's Programming has significant impacts on our Awakened Mindset. We are constantly influenced by music in ways we don't realize, leading us to feel, think, and act in accordance with external programming rather than our own conscious will. While music can be a tool for positive emotional regulation, relying on it to constantly shift mood can also prevent us from fully processing our authentic emotions or developing internal coping mechanisms. Music's ability to create associations and influence mood is heavily exploited by industries, programming our desires and purchasing habits. Moreover, music can create powerful emotional states that may not align with objective reality, leading to a romanticized view of certain behaviors, lifestyles, or even historical events. Finally, music can reinforce other existing programs, such as the need for external validation (e.g., through songs about fame, popularity, or seeking approval) or desensitization (through repeated exposure to violent or explicit lyrical themes)

6. Entertainment:
The Alluring Programmer

As we continue to peel back the layers of societal programming, we encounter an extremely powerful force, Entertainment. Often dismissed as mere leisure or escapism, entertainment in its myriad forms, from movies and television to video games, music, and social media content, is a sophisticated programmer of our minds. It operates through immersion, emotional resonance, and repeated exposure, shaping our perceptions, values, and behaviors in ways we rarely consciously detect. Entertainment's programming power lies in its ability to engage our emotions and bypass our critical faculties, creating a fertile ground for the absorption of ideas and behaviors.

Entertainment excels at eliciting and managing our emotional states. Through carefully crafted narratives, compelling visuals, evocative music, and dynamic pacing, movies, shows, and games can induce joy, fear, excitement, sadness, or anger. This emotional engagement is not just for pleasure; it's a powerful conditioning tool. When specific ideas, lifestyles, or behaviors are consistently paired with positive or negative emotional experiences within entertainment, our brains form strong associations. For instance, a character who embodies a certain trait (e.g., aggression, consumerism, or a particular political view) might be consistently portrayed as heroic or desirable, programming us to associate that trait with positive feelings and aspirations. Conversely, undesirable traits or characters can be linked to negative emotions, creating aversion. This emotional conditioning happens beneath conscious awareness, making the programmed associations feel like natural inclinations rather than external influences.

One of entertainment's most potent programming functions is the normalization of behaviors and ideas. Through repeated exposure, what might initially seem shocking, extreme, or unusual gradually becomes familiar, then acceptable, and eventually, even desirable. This is a form of desensitization, where our emotional and critical filters are slowly worn down. For example, the constant portrayal of certain body types, consumer habits, or interpersonal dynamics in popular media can shift societal norms, making these representations appear "normal" or aspirational, even if they are unrealistic or unhealthy. Similarly, complex social or political issues can be simplified or framed in specific ways within entertainment narratives, programming audiences to adopt particular viewpoints without deep critical engagement. The more we see something, the less we question it, and the more likely we are to integrate it into our understanding of the world.

Entertainment provides powerful narratives that serve as blueprints for understanding reality. Stories are fundamental to human cognition, and the stories we consume through entertainment actively shape our beliefs about ourselves, others, and the world. From archetypal heroes and villains to depictions of success, failure, relationships, and societal structures, entertainment offers models for behavior and belief systems. These narratives can program us with specific ideas about what is right or wrong, what is possible or impossible, and what really matters in life. For instance, a show might consistently portray a certain type of wealth as the ultimate goal, or a particular form of conflict resolution as the only effective one. Over time, these narrative patterns can become deeply ingrained beliefs, influencing our decisions and actions in real life.

Beyond active influence, entertainment also programs us through distraction and escapism. In a world that can often feel overwhelming or uncomfortable, entertainment offers a readily available escape. While escapism can be a healthy coping mechanism in moderation, its constant availability and allure can program a habit of disengagement from real-world problems, personal introspection, or challenging realities. When faced with discomfort, the programmed response might be to "tune out" with a show, a game, or endless scrolling, rather than to confront, process, or act. This passive consumption keeps us in a state of comfortable distraction, preventing the deeper self-inquiry and critical observation necessary for an Awakened Mindset. It's a program that prioritizes comfort overgrowth, and superficial engagement over profound understanding.

Entertainment is inextricably linked to consumer culture, acting as a powerful programmer of desires. Product placement, aspirational lifestyles portrayed in media, and the constant showcasing of new technologies or fashion trends program us to want specific goods and services. Characters we admire use certain brands, live in certain types of homes, or engage in certain leisure activities, creating a subconscious link between these external markers and the feelings of happiness, success, or belonging that the entertainment evokes. This programming fuels consumerism, driving us to seek external fulfillment through acquisition, often without questioning the true source of our desires or whether these acquisitions genuinely align with our deeper values.

The nature of entertainment's programming has significant impacts on our Awakened Mindset, often keeping us tethered to unconscious patterns. We become accustomed to passively receiving information and emotional cues, reducing our capacity for active engagement, critical analysis, and independent thought. Entertainment often presents highly curated, exaggerated, or simplified versions of reality. When this becomes our primary input, our understanding of the world can become skewed, making it harder to navigate complex real-life situations or empathize with diverse experiences. The immersive and emotionally engaging nature of entertainment can bypass our logical filters, making us less likely to question narratives, identify biases, or discern truth from fiction. We absorb the programming without conscious scrutiny. Entertainment frequently reinforces other existing programs, such as the need for External Validation (through celebrity culture and social media performance), or Desensitization (through repeated exposure to violence, superficiality, or extreme behaviors). It can perpetuate cycles of comparison, anxiety, and unfulfilling pursuits.

Chapter 11

April Fools: The Architecture of the Joke

1. The Ritual of the Fool

We open this section on April 1st because it is the "Ground Zero" of the Mental Matrix. To "April Fool" someone is to lead them down a path of false belief for the amusement and profit of the one holding the script. This section isn't just about societal habits; it is about the specific, calculated deceptions that have made "Fools" of us all.

The tradition of April Fool's Day likely began as a way to mock those who refused to switch from the Julian (natural) calendar to the Gregorian (corporate) calendar. Those who still celebrated the New Year in April, aligned with the "opening" of the Earth, were labeled fools by the new authority. We have been programmed to laugh at the very people who were trying to stay connected to the truth. By reclaiming this day, we stop being the punchline of the joke and start becoming the authors of the reality.

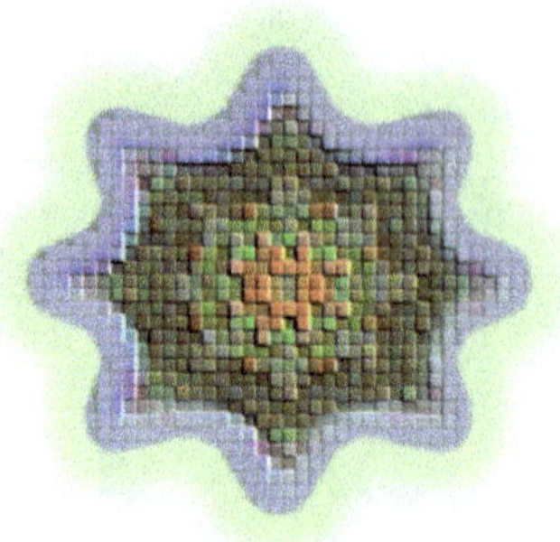

2. The Three Pillars of the Fool

2.1. The Temporal Fool: The Calendar Hijack

Before we lived by the clock, we lived by the Earth. Historically, the "New Year" was a celebration of the Spring Equinox, the moment life literally "opens" (Aperire) also known as April. In the 1500s, Pope Gregory XIII introduced the Gregorian calendar, a calculated shift that moved the New Year to the dead of winter. This wasn't just a change in dates; it was a psychological realignment. By starting the year in January, the system forced humanity to attempt "new beginnings" while the natural world was still in hibernation, creating a permanent state of biological lag.

The word calendar itself reveals the true intent as it stems from kalendarium, the Roman ledger used to track monthly debts and interest payments. By standardizing time into rigid, artificial blocks, the Matrix transformed our experience of life into a series of billable hours and tax cycles. We stopped measuring time by the growth of a garden and started measuring it by the "due date" of a loan. This creates temporal anxiety, the constant, low-level fear that you are behind on a schedule you never agreed to.

The first deception was taking your time. By moving the start of the year to January, the system ensured you would always be out of sync with your biology. You are fooled into setting goals in the dark of winter and paying debts on a schedule designed by Roman accountants. You are living in a time-signature that doesn't belong to you.

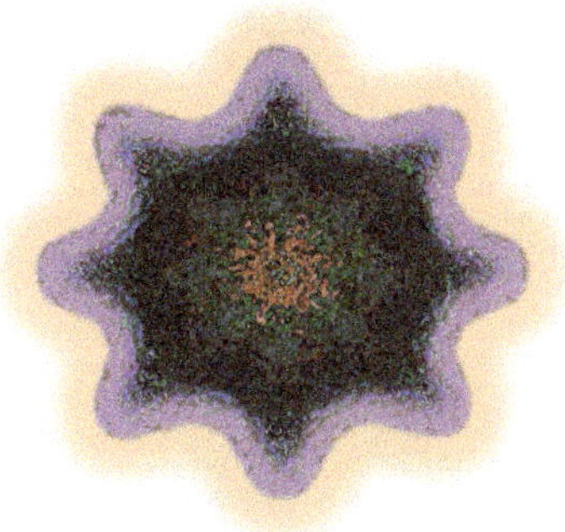

2.2. The Spiritual Fool: The Mandate of Fear

Most modern religious doctrines operate on a "Root Program" of violence disguised as justice. When we are taught that the Creator is a judge who demands blood or sacrifice to be satisfied. Meanwhile, we are being programmed to accept authority figures who use the same methods. This imperial logic mirrors the military, it values obedience over empathy. If the highest power in the universe is a violent, punishing God, then human wars, capital punishment, and systemic cruelty become "holy" by extension.

True creation is an act of nurturance, not destruction. As a mother knows, you do not create life to "test" it or to demand its sacrifice; you create to sustain. When we unplug from the "Punisher" narrative, we realize that the Light inside us is not a gift from a distant, angry judge, but a natural inheritance from a Creator that functions like a life-giving sun. By rejecting the mandate of fear, we strip the Authority Matrix of its greatest weapon as the threat of a spiritual executioner.

The second deception was taking your divinity. You were fooled into believing that the Creator is a "God" who requires blood, sacrifice, and external rituals to be appeased. This program keeps you looking at a book for permission to be good, while the Light you seek is already encoded in your DNA. It is the ultimate prank that convinced the owner of the house that they have to pay rent to a stranger to live there.

2.3. The Tribal Fool: The Box of Isolation

For the vast majority of human history, the Tribe was our survival technology. We lived in circles, sharing the burdens of childcare, cooking, and eldercare across generations. The Matrix dismantled the tribe and replaced it with the "Nuclear Family", a small, isolated "box" that is easier to control and more expensive to maintain. By programming us to move away from our kin as soon as we reach adulthood, the system severs our natural safety net, making us dependent on corporations for our needs and the state for our security.

The push for "individualism" is actually a profit strategy. One tribe needs one set of tools; thirty isolated families need thirty of everything. This separation creates a "Loneliness Economy," where we spend our lives working to pay for services (like daycare and nursing homes) that our ancestors provided for each other for free. Reclaiming your family and your community isn't just a sentimental act; it is an economic and spiritual rebellion. It is a refusal to let the Matrix profit from your isolation.

The third deception was taking your community. You were fooled into believing that independence meant living in a tiny, isolated box, disconnected from your family and your elders. The Fool works forty hours a week to pay someone else to watch their children and someone else to care for their parents. The system sold you "freedom" but delivered a "subscription to survival."

"The Awakened Mindset: The Epistemic Ripple Effect" shines a light on the often-unseen programming shaping our thoughts, from fear-driven narratives to societal pressures.

I equip you with Epistemic Principles and Mindful Practices to design a Knowledge Architecture that fosters clarity, wisdom, and inner strength.

My Vision is to spark an Epistemic Ripple Effect – each Awakened Mindset contributing to a wave of positive change, building a future where unity and understanding become the cornerstones of our shared world.

Part 3: Breaking Free

Chapter 12
The Journey to the Awakened Mindset

We are born different on purpose, to make up a piece of a universal puzzle. No two puzzle pieces are the same size or shape, or it would not be a puzzle. Your inherent worth and value isn't contingent on performance, conformity, or external validation. Your value is intrinsic, baked into your very DNA, into the unique shape of your "puzzle piece." Your authentic purpose and unique design aren't accidental; it's necessary. Your "lost art," your specific skills, talents, perspectives, and even quirks, are precisely what's needed to complete the larger picture. Illustrating that diversity isn't just a buzzword; it's the very foundation of strength and completion. A puzzle made of identical pieces isn't a puzzle at all; it's a monochrome slab. True richness and coherence come from the harmonious fit of distinct parts. Your piece is meant to be uniquely shaped, then comparing it to another piece becomes utterly illogical and pointless. This alone is a profound antidote to Performance Pressure and the endless cycle of Consumer Culture's demands for conformity.

We all have different DNA for a reason, and that is because we are supposed to be different to be a piece of the universal puzzle. However, it often seems everyone wants to be the same.

This is a direct result of how the 4 D's keep you from our authentic self. The constant noise and external stimulation of the Algorithm Mind and Consumer Culture keep us so busy looking outward and chasing artificial ideals that we rarely have the stillness to look inward and recognize our own unique blueprint. We're too distracted by what everyone else seems to be or have, to even notice our own inherent shape. The programmed mindset disengages us from our authentic selves. We're taught to fit molds, to conform to cultural, academic, or professional expectations, rather than exploring our genuine inclinations. We become disengaged from the intuition that whispers our unique purpose.

When everyone is performing and conforming, genuine connection is difficult. We disengage from the empathy needed to celebrate others' uniqueness, often viewing it with suspicion or envy because our own sense of self is fragile. This is perhaps the most insidious aspect. Society, through its programming, actively disarms our individuality and authenticity. Performance Pressure and Consumer Culture disarm our sense of intrinsic worth, teaching us that our value is conditional on external metrics or material possessions, not on our unique being. This makes us fear standing out, eroding our self-worth.

The Fear Factor and Hate Cycle often target those who are "different." This pressure to conform disarms our courage to express our unique voice, to deviate from the norm, for fear of rejection, ridicule, or even ostracization. The educational and professional systems often prioritize conformity and adherence to established rules over genuine creativity and unique problem-solving, effectively disarming our innate drive to express our distinct "puzzle piece."

The ultimate consequence of the 4 D's is the attempt to Destroy the very fabric of individuality that makes the "universal puzzle" vibrant. Rigid cultural programming, fueled by fear and hate, seeks to destroy anything that doesn't fit its narrow definitions, leading to suppression of diverse expressions, perspectives, and ways of being. When everyone strives to be the same, true innovation, authentic connection, and societal resilience suffer. It leads to a fragile monoculture that is easily exploited and lacks the adaptability that true diversity provides.

To shed the layers of programming, the expectations of conformity, and the fear of being "different," and instead, to truly see and embrace the unique shape of your own puzzle piece. To reconnect with the intuition and inner wisdom that guides you to express your authentic self, rather than being driven by external metrics or societal pressures. To understand that the world doesn't need more identical pieces; it needs your unique piece to fit perfectly with all the other unique pieces, fostering empathy, curiosity, and genuine collaboration, breaking down the very barriers of that keep us programmed.

1. Quantum Consciousness: The Fabric of Reality and Awareness

As we shift our focus from the intricate architecture of programming to the profound mechanisms of breaking free, we arrive at the frontier where science and spirituality seemingly merge, Quantum Consciousness. This concept suggests that consciousness is not merely a product of our physical brain, but rather a fundamental, intrinsic property of the universe itself, deeply intertwined with the range and profound principles of quantum mechanics.

Briefly, Quantum Consciousness posits that our individual awareness is connected to a universal field of consciousness, operating at a subatomic, non-local level. It draws parallels between the observer effect in quantum physics (where the act of observation influences reality) and the profound power of human consciousness to shape our experience. It suggests that our perceptions, thoughts, and intentions are not isolated events within our skulls, but rather active participants in the very unfolding of reality. Understanding Quantum Consciousness is an invitation to recognize that our minds are not purely passive recipients of programmed data, but dynamic, interconnected forces capable of influencing and creating our perceived world, offering a powerful pathway to transcend the limitations of the "Subconscious Prison" and fully embrace the boundless potential of the Awakened Mindset.

2. Christ Consciousness: The Embodied Freedom Beyond Programming

Christ Consciousness represents a state of profound spiritual awakening, a universal awareness characterized by unconditional love, radical self-realization, and an intrinsic understanding of unity that transcends ego and separation. Within the framework of this book, attaining this state is not a religious decree, but the ultimate fruit of dismantling the Programmed Perspectives and escaping the Subconscious Prison.

Each act of identifying and detaching from the artificial constructs of the Mental Matrix, be it the Imperfection Trap, the Fear Factor, or the limiting narratives of societal roles peel away a layer of illusion. This continuous de-programming reveals the Authentic Self, an inner essence inherently aligned with the qualities of Christ Consciousness, boundless compassion, unshakeable peace, and the profound wisdom that suffering is a choice. It is through this inner liberation that individuals access a higher truth, moving beyond the fragmented reality imposed by external conditioning to embody a unified, loving awareness that recollects "who they were supposed to be" all along.

3. Quantum Consciousness and Christ Consciousness: The Unified Field of Liberation

At the very heart of the Awakened Mindset lies a profound convergence, where the deepest scientific inquiries into reality meet the most elevated spiritual truths, the interconnectedness of Quantum Consciousness and Christ Consciousness. If Quantum Consciousness posits that our individual awareness is inextricably woven into the fundamental fabric of the universe, a universal field where the act of observation can indeed influence the very nature of reality, then Christ Consciousness represents the pinnacle expression of that universal awareness, embodying a state of radical self-realization, unconditional love, and profound unity. This isn't merely a philosophical abstraction; it is the ultimate blueprint for breaking free from the Subconscious Prison. As we de-program the limiting beliefs and engineered divisions that separate us from our Authentic Self, we begin to perceive and engage with this unified field.

Our individual consciousness, no longer tethered by the illusions of the Mental Matrix, becomes a deliberate co-creator, aligning its vibratory essence with the expansive, loving, and interconnected intelligence that both quantum mechanics and spiritual masters describe. This realization empowers us to not only transcend fabricated suffering, but to consciously participate in the ongoing creation of a reality rooted in compassion, wisdom, and the boundless potential of our true, unified essence.

4. Consciousness and Conscience:
Pillars of the Awakened Mindset

In the journey toward the Awakened Mindset, the delicate distinction between consciousness and conscience becomes profoundly illuminated. True consciousness is the very act of waking up, the acute, deliberate awareness of the intricate Mental Matrix that has been programmed into your being, allowing you to perceive the unseen walls of the Subconscious Prison. This newfound clarity is not merely intellectual; it is a fundamental shift in perception that enables you to observe the narratives, rules, and conditioned responses that have dictated your reality. With this expanded consciousness, the individual then gains the capacity to examine their **conscience**, that inner arbiter of right and wrong, often deeply impressed by societal, religious, or familial programming.

A programmed conscience might inflict shame for authentic self-expression (the Imperfection Trap) or guilt for stepping outside prescribed roles (like those in Disney narratives), even if those roles contradict genuine well-being. However, through the lens of awakened consciousness, one can begin to discern the authentic promptings of a pure conscience, aligned with universal wisdom and Christ Consciousness, from the internalized dictates of conditional worth. This pivotal process allows for the liberation of the moral compass, empowering the individual to act not from programmed fear or external validation, but from the profound inner knowing that guides them toward their Authentic Self and true inner peace.

5. Consciousness and Deep Focus:
Cultivating Intentional Presence

The relationship between consciousness and deep focus is symbiotic. Your ability to enter a state of deep focus is a direct measure of your capacity to harness your consciousness. If consciousness is your broad, perceptive awareness, the ability to see and understand the elements of your Mental Matrix, and the programming that shapes your reality, then deep focus is the intentional application and narrowing of that awareness onto a singular task or purpose.

It is the moment you consciously direct your internal resources, cutting through the constant noise and fragmented attention that the Subconscious Prison and its various distraction mechanisms constantly generate. This intentional channeling of consciousness is not just about productivity; it is a profound act of self-reclamation, asserting mastery over your own attention and, by extension, your own creative power within the quantum field.

Deep focus, often referred to as the "Flow State" (a concept pioneered by psychologist Mihaly Csikszentmihalyi), is a powerful psychological and neurological mechanism for optimal engagement and performance. It's that coveted "in the zone" feeling where distractions fade, time seems to warp, and you become completely absorbed in the task at hand. It begins with a deliberate commitment to a single, clearly defined task. This initial conscious choice is paramount, signaling to the brain to allocate all available cognitive resources. The task must be challenging enough to be engaging, but not so difficult as to cause frustration or anxiety. There's a sweet spot where your skills are perfectly matched to the demands, pushing you just enough to stay fully absorbed without feeling overwhelmed. This dynamic equilibrium keeps the brain stimulated and motivated.

When you enter deep focus, your brain undergoes a mere but significant shift. Activity in certain areas of the prefrontal cortex, the part of the brain responsible for self-monitoring, self-consciousness, and mind-wandering (the "Default Mode Network"), temporarily decreases. This "transient hypo-frontality", the part of the brain that is in control of higher-order thinking, allows the brain to quiet internal chatter, reduce self-criticism, and filter out external distractions, creating a clear channel for the task at hand. The brain releases a potent cocktail of neurochemicals, including dopamine (for motivation and reward), norepinephrine (for alertness and attention), serotonin (for mood stabilization), and endorphins (for feelings of well-being).

This biochemical surge enhances focus, provides sustained energy, and makes the experience intrinsically rewarding, encouraging you to stay in the state. In deep focus, the gap between your thoughts and actions shrinks. You are not consciously deliberating every move; rather, the action itself feels effortless and spontaneous. This "automaticity" allows for highly efficient processing and execution. Because you are so deeply absorbed, your subjective experience of time can dramatically shift. Minutes can feel like seconds, and hours can fly by unnoticed.

Cultivating deep focus is a powerful tool for de-programming Distraction and reclaiming your mental sovereignty. It is a practice of intentionally applying your Awakened Mindset to manifest real-world results, reinforcing the idea that your consciousness, when deliberately directed, possesses immense power to shape your experience and dismantle the walls of your Subconscious Prison.

Chapter 13
The Techniques for Awakening Your Mindset

1. The Arsenal to Liberation: Techniques for Combating Negative Programming

Having explored deep focus as a powerful application of consciousness, a means to cut through the pervasive distraction and intentionally direct your mental energy, we now pivot to a crucial set of practical tools for active de-programming. This refined capacity for sustained awareness is not simply for productivity; it is the fundamental prerequisite for engaging the sophisticated techniques necessary to combat negative programming. Just as deep focus allows you to meticulously examine a task, it enables you to consciously observe the devious walls of your Subconscious Prison and identify the specific negative programs embedded within your Mental Matrix. Methods such as Mindfulness Meditation, Cognitive Behavioral Therapy (CBT), and Neuro-Linguistic Programming (NLP) provide a structured and potent arsenal, each offering distinct pathways to challenge, reframe, and ultimately dismantle the limiting beliefs and automatic responses that hold you captive.

The journey to liberation from deeply ingrained negative programming requires more than just awareness; it demands active intervention and consistent practice. The techniques for combating negative programming are designed to systematically identify, challenge, and re-pattern the limiting beliefs, distorted perceptions, and automatic emotional responses that keep you bound. Broadly, these methods aim to heighten self-awareness by recognizing the precise triggers and internal dialogues initiated by negative programs. Challenge programmed beliefs by critically questioning the validity and utility of long-held assumptions and fears.

Reframe perspectives by consciously shifting interpretations of events and self-narratives from disempowering to empowering, re-patterned responses to break automatic, unhelpful reactions and cultivate new, more authentic and beneficial thought and behavior patterns. These techniques, individually and in combination, provide the practical "how-to" for actively dismantling the Subconscious Prison and reclaiming your Authentic Self.

2. Mindfulness Meditation:
Practices for Reprogramming Your Mindset

Mindfulness Meditation cultivates present moment awareness without judgment, allowing you to observe and detach from programmed thoughts and emotional patterns.

Mindful Awareness Meditation

- **Observation (10–20 Minutes):** Sit comfortably. Open your attention to everything that arises sounds, physical sensations, feelings, and especially thoughts. Acknowledge each element (e.g., "A thought about dinner," "Sound of traffic," "Feeling of tightness") without engaging it. Let it pass.
    - How it Helps: Develops the ability to observe thoughts, emotions, and sensations as they arise without getting carried away by them, creating space to recognize programmed patterns.

Body Scan Meditation

- **Physical Sensation** (15-30 Minutes): Lie on your back. Begin by bringing your awareness to your toes. Slowly, and deliberately, move your attention upward, to the feet, ankles, lower legs, etc., until you reach the top of your head.
    - How it Helps: Increases awareness of physical sensations, allowing you to notice how programmed stress or anxiety might manifest in the body and providing an opportunity to respond with compassion rather than reactivity.

Mindful Breathing

- **The Breath (5-10 Minutes):** Choose a single point of sensation for the breath (the nostrils, the chest, or the rising and falling of the abdomen). Focus all attention on the sensation of the air moving in and out at that point.
    - How it Helps: Provides a consistent anchor to the present moment, helping to interrupt cycles of rumination on programmed thoughts and bringing you back to a state of calm observation.

Mindful Observation

- **Sensory Input (5-15 Minutes):** Choose an object (a cup of coffee, a tree outside the window, your hand). Observe it as if you have never seen it before. Note its color, texture, light reflection, shape, and unique properties.
    - How it Helps: Encourages paying attention to sensory experiences without labeling or judgment, fostering a more objective view of reality that can challenge programmed biases and assumptions.

Loving-Kindness Meditation (Metta)

- **Compassionate Intention (10-20 minutes):** Systematically send phrases of goodwill (e.g., "May you be safe. May you be happy. May you live with ease.") to five targets: 1) Yourself, 2) A close loved one, 3) A neutral acquaintance, 4) A difficult person (optional), and 5) All beings universally.
    - How it Helps: Cultivates feelings of warmth, kindness, and compassion towards yourself and others, counteracting programming that might lead to self-criticism or negativity towards others.

Walking Meditation

- **Movement (10-30 Minutes):** Focus all attention on the sensations in your feet and legs as you walk. Notice the lifting of the heel, the slight shift of weight, the placement of the foot, and the contact with the ground. Walk slower than usual
    - How it Helps: Brings mindful awareness to the physical act of walking, grounding you in the present moment and providing a different way to observe your thoughts without getting entangled in them. It interrupts the mind's tendency to run internal narratives (NATs) during automated activities like walking.

3. CBT Techniques for Reprogramming: Your Simple Guide

Cognitive Behavioral Therapy (CBT) is a practical approach that helps you understand the connection between your thoughts, feelings, and behaviors. The core idea is that our thoughts significantly influence how we feel and act.

Think of CBT as learning to become a detective for your own thinking patterns. It gives you tools to identify unhelpful thoughts (often stemming from programming), challenge their accuracy, and change them to improve how you feel and what you do.

Here are some key CBT techniques focusing on how they help you reprogram your mindset:

A. Identifying Negative Automatic Thoughts (NATs): Catching the Quick Thoughts

- Simple Idea: NATs are those rapid, often negative thoughts that pop into your head automatically in response to a situation. They're like quick, uninvited guests in your mind. They often reflect your underlying, programmed beliefs.

- How it Helps with Programming: Programming instills automatic ways of thinking. Identifying NATs helps you become aware of these programmed thought patterns that run on autopilot. You can't change a thought you don't realize you're having.

- Simple Example:
  - Situation: You get constructive criticism at work.
  - NAT (Programmed): "I'm terrible at my job. I'm going to get fired." (This thought pops up automatically, likely linked to programming around performance pressure or fear of failure).

B. Challenging Negative Thoughts: Questioning the Evidence

- Simple Idea: Once you've identified a negative thought, challenging it means questioning its accuracy and validity. You act like a detective, looking for evidence for and against the thought.

- How it Helps with Programming: Programmed beliefs often feel like absolute truths, even if they're not based on reality. Challenging these thoughts helps you see the flaws in the programming by examining the actual evidence. It weakens the thought's power.

- Simple Example:
    - Negative Thought: "I'm terrible at my job. I'm going to get fired."
    - Challenging Questions: "What is the actual evidence that I'm terrible at my job? (List successes, positive feedback). What is the evidence against this thought? (List areas for improvement, but also things, done well). Is this thought 100% true? What's a more balanced way to look at this?"

C. Cognitive Restructuring: Rewriting the Thought

- Simple Idea: After challenging a negative thought and seeing its flaws, cognitive restructuring is the process of creating and adopting a more balanced, realistic, or helpful alternative thought. It's actively rewriting the script in your mind.

- How it Helps with Programming: This is where you actively replace the old, programmed thought with a new, chosen one. You're building new neural pathways and training your brain to think in a different, more constructive way, directly counteracting the old programming.

- Simple Example:
    - Old Negative Thought: "I'm terrible at my job. I'm going to get fired."
    - New Restructured Thought: "Okay, I received some feedback on this project, and there are areas I can improve. I'm still learning, and this feedback will help me get better. I'm capable of doing good work."

D. Behavioral Experiments: Testing Your Beliefs in Real Life

- Simple Idea: This involves treating a programmed belief or fear as a hypothesis and testing it out in a real-life situation to see if it holds true.

- How it Helps with Programming: Programmed fears and beliefs often lead to avoidance behaviors that prevent you from gathering evidence that contradicts the programming. Behavioral experiments help you safely confront these fears and gather real-world data that can dismantle the programmed belief.

- Simple Example:
    - Programmed Belief/Fear (e.g., from social programming): "If I speak up in a meeting, people will think I'm stupid." (This belief leads to avoiding speaking).
    - Behavioral Experiment: Plan to make one brief, prepared comment in the next meeting. After the meeting, observe what actually happened. Did people react negatively? Did anyone comment? What is the evidence from the actual experience? (Often, the feared outcome doesn't happen, providing evidence against the programmed belief).

E. Thought Records: Your Detective's Notebook

- Simple Idea: A thought record is a structured way to write down a situation, the feelings it triggered, the negative automatic thoughts that arose, the evidence for and against those thoughts, and the restructured, more balanced thought.

- How it Helps with Programming: This technique provides a systematic process for uncovering and challenging programmed thoughts regularly. By writing it down, you make the unconscious programming conscious and apply the steps of challenging and restructuring, reinforcing the reprogramming process over time. It's like keeping a log of the old programs you are finding and the new ones you are installing.

Anchoring the Practice: Your CBT Motivational Acronym

C.H.A.N.G.E.

C - Catch your thoughts (Identify NATs)

H - Handle your thoughts (Question the Evidence)

A - Act (Do Behavioral Experiments)

N - Note your thoughts (Use Thought Records)

G- Generate new thoughts (Cognitive Restructure)

E - Evaluate the results (See how changing thoughts impacts feelings/behaviors)

This acronym guides you through the core steps of using CBT to identify and change programmed thinking. These CBT techniques provide a powerful, structured way to work with the cognitive aspects of programming. By consistently applying them, you can actively rewrite the unhelpful thought patterns that have been running in your subconscious.

4. NLP Techniques for Reprogramming: Your Simple Guide

Neuro-Linguistic Programming (NLP) is like a user manual for your brain. It helps you understand how your mind processes information, communicates with itself and others, and how you can make changes to improve your thoughts, feelings, and behaviors. Think of it as learning the "language" your brain uses so you can talk to it more effectively and update its old "programs."

Here are some key NLP techniques focusing on how they help you reprogram your mindset:

A. Reframing: Changing the Picture

- Simple Idea: Reframing is about looking at the same situation, thought, or belief from a different angle or giving it a new meaning. It's like taking a picture and putting a different frame around it – the picture is the same, but the way you see it changes.
- How it Helps with Programming: Programmed beliefs and experiences often have a fixed, negative "frame" around them. Reframing helps you break free from that fixed view and see alternative possibilities or more empowering meanings. It can turn a perceived obstacle into a challenge, or a past "failure" into a learning opportunity.
- Simple Example:
    - Old Frame (Programmed): "I made a mistake on that project. I'm a failure." (This thought is framed as a judgment of your entire self).
    - New Frame (Reframed): "I made a mistake on that project. That's a chance to learn exactly what went wrong so I can do better next time." (The same event is now framed as a learning experience).

B. Anchoring: Setting Your Emotional Triggers

- Simple Idea: Anchoring creates a specific trigger (like touching your finger and thumb together, or a specific word) that is linked to a particular feeling or state (like confidence, calm, or focus). It's like setting a mental "button" you can press to instantly access a desired feeling.
- How it Helps with Programming: Programmed experiences often create unwanted anchors, triggers that automatically set off negative feelings (e.g., thinking about public speaking automatically triggers anxiety). Anchoring allows you to create new, positive anchors to access resourceful states when you need them, or to neutralize old, negative anchors.
- Simple Example:
  - Creating a Positive Anchor: Remember a time you felt incredibly confident. As you fully re-experience that feeling, squeeze your left earlobe (or choose any unique physical action). Repeat this a few times. Now, squeezing your earlobe can become an "anchor" to access that feeling of confidence when you need it.
  - Using it for Programming: If a programmed situation (like receiving criticism) usually triggers feelings of inadequacy, you can consciously fire your "confidence anchor" to access a more resourceful state instead of the automatic programmed response.

C. Visualization: Using Your Mind's Eye

- Simple Idea: Visualization is using your imagination to vividly create mental pictures, sounds, and feelings of a desired outcome, state, or experience. It's like running a movie in your mind.
- How it Helps with Programming: Your subconscious mind often doesn't distinguish between a vividly imagined experience and a real one. You can use visualization to "install" new, positive "programs" by mentally rehearsing desired behaviors,

outcomes, or feelings, overriding old limiting beliefs or fears. It helps the subconscious become familiar and comfortable with new possibilities.

- Simple Example:
  - Overcoming Programmed Fear: If you have a programmed fear of public speaking, visualize yourself confidently walking onto the stage, feeling calm and capable, seeing the audience engaged, and hearing the sound of your clear voice. Do this regularly to reprogram the fear response.
  - Installing a New Belief: If you have programmed belief, you're not creative, visualize yourself easily coming up with new ideas, feeling inspired, and successfully creating something you're proud of.

D. The Meta Model: Questioning Your Language

- Simple Idea: The Meta Model is a set of specific questions designed to challenge vague or limiting language (yours and others'). It helps you get to the specific details and meanings behind words, uncovering hidden assumptions and distortions.
- How it Helps with Programming: Programmed beliefs are often embedded in generalized or distorted language ("Everyone thinks I'm incompetent," "I can never do anything right," "It's impossible"). The Meta Model helps you unpack these vague statements, revealing the lack of specific evidence or the underlying illogical assumptions, thereby weakening the programmed belief.
- Simple Example:
  - Programmed Statement: "Everyone thinks I'm incompetent." (This is a generalization and a mind-read).
  - Meta Model Questions: "Everyone? Who specifically thinks you're incompetent?" "How do you know what *everyone* thinks?" "What specifically makes you think you are

incompetent?" (These questions challenge the generalization and mind-read, forcing the subconscious to look for specific evidence, which is often lacking).

E. Perceptual Positions: Stepping into Different Shoes

- Simple Idea: This technique involves consciously experiencing a situation from different viewpoints:
  - 1st Position: Your own perspective (seeing, hearing, feeling from your own body).
  - 2nd Position: Another person's perspective (imagining you are them, seeing, hearing, feeling as if you were in their body).
  - 3rd Position: An objective observer's perspective (watching the interaction from the outside, like watching a movie). Third Person Perspective is key to being able to see things differently.
- How it Helps with Programming: Programmed responses often lock us into a single, rigid perspective (usually 1st position, driven by our own programmed emotions and beliefs). Stepping into 2nd and 3rd positions helps you gain new insights, understand the situation more fully, reduce programmed biases (like judgment or blame), and find more resourceful ways to respond.
- Simple Example:
  - Dealing with Conflict (Programmed Response: Anger/Blame): If you're programmed to react with anger when there's conflict, after the event, mentally step into 2nd position (the other person's shoes).
  - Imagine their perspective, their potential fears or intentions. Then step into 3rd position (the observer) to see the interaction objectively. This can reveal that the conflict wasn't just about you, breaking the programmed blame cycle,

F. Submodalities: The Building Blocks of Experience

- Simple Idea: Submodalities are the smaller sensory details that make up our internal experiences (visual: brightness, size, location; auditory: volume, tone, speed; kinesthetic: temperature, pressure, texture). They are the "code" of your internal representations.

- How it Helps with Programming: The emotional intensity and impact of a programmed thought, memory, or belief are encoded in its submodalities. A fearful memory might be a large, bright, close-up picture with loud sounds and intense physical feelings. A limiting belief might feel "heavy" or be associated with a dull, distant image. By consciously changing the submodalities of an internal representation, you can change its emotional impact and reprogram your response.

- Simple Example:

    - Reducing a Fearful Memory (Programmed Fear): Take a fearful memory (programmed fear). Notice its submodalities (e.g., Is the image big or small? Bright or dim? Close or far?). Now, consciously change them. Make the image smaller, dimmer, push it further away, turn the color black and white, turn down the sound. Notice how changing these submodalities reduces the emotional intensity of the programmed fear response linked to that memory.

Anchoring the Practice: Your NLP Motivational Acronym

R.E.W.I.R.E.

R - Reframing:
Change your perspective

E - Exploring:
Use Meta Model to question and explore the details

W - Witnessing:
Use Perceptual Positions to see from different views

I - Imagining:
Use Visualization to create new possibilities

R - Resetting:
Use Anchoring to access resourceful states

E - Editing:
Use Submodalities to change the feeling of experiences

This acronym is easy to remember and encapsulates the active process of changing your internal programming. These techniques, when practiced consistently, provide powerful ways to interact directly with the subconscious mind and reprogram the limiting patterns and beliefs that have been installed over time. They give you a practical "user manual" for your brain, empowering you to take control of your inner world.

Part 4
Subconscious Audit: Plan of Action for Reprogramming

Chapter 14

The Audit of Your Inner World

This plan outlines actionable steps for each core aspect of the subconscious, guiding you through the "audit" (uncovering old programming) and the "rewiring" (installing new, empowering programs). Each step integrates techniques from Mindfulness, Cognitive Behavioral Therapy (CBT), and Neuro-Linguistic Programming (NLP).

1. The Archive of Experiences: The Data Bank: Where Your Past Lives

This aspect stores all your memories, interpretations, and associated emotions. Negative programming often stems from emotionally charged past experiences or repetitive inputs.

I. Audit Phase: Uncovering Programmed Memories/Interpretations

- **Goal:** Identify influential memories and their existing interpretations that contribute to limiting perceptions.
- **Actionable Steps:**

A. **Mindful Reflection (Mindfulness):** Dedicate quiet time to sit with and observe recurring intrusive memories, or memories that consistently evoke strong negative emotions. Don't judge them, just notice their content and the feelings they bring up.

B. **Memory Journaling (CBT):** Pick a specific memory that feels "stuck" or painful. Write down the event, your immediate thoughts, and feelings. Then, write down the interpretation you *currently* hold about that memory (e.g., "This memory proves I'm always inadequate").

C. **Meta-Model Questioning (NLP):** Apply Meta-Model questions to your written interpretation of the memory. "Who specifically said that?" "What exactly happened?" "How do you know that proves [negative interpretation]?" "What was *not* said or done?" This helps challenge generalizations and distortions in the stored interpretation.

II. Reprogramming Phase: Rewiring the Impact of Past Experiences

- **Goal:** Reduce the negative emotional charge of past memories and reinterpret them in more empowering ways, shifting your current perception.
- **Actionable Steps:**

  A. **Mindful Re-observation (Mindfulness):** With the identified memory, practice observing it from a detached, third-person perspective (like watching a movie of yourself). Notice the emotions without getting swept away. Just observe the memory as an event that *happened*, not something that *is* happening now.

  B. **Cognitive Restructuring for Memories (CBT):** Re-examine your journaled memory. Challenge the initial interpretation: "Is there any alternative way to view this event?" "What did I learn from it?" "How did I grow *because* of it?" Rewrite the memory's narrative with a more balanced and empowering interpretation.

  C. **Submodalities Shift (NLP):** As you hold the memory image in your mind, consciously change its submodalities. Make it smaller, dimmer, move it further away, change it to black and white, or remove any associated sounds. Then, envision a new, positive interpretation of the memory and make that new image bright, large, and close.

2. The Pattern Recognition & Automation Engine: The Habit Maker: Your Autopilot

This aspect turns repeated behaviors, thoughts, and emotional responses into automatic habits to save energy. Negative programming often manifests as unhelpful automated patterns.

I. Audit Phase: Uncovering Programmed Habits

- **Goal:** Identify specific automated behaviors, thoughts, or emotional sequences that are limiting or unhelpful.
- **Actionable Steps:**

A. **Mindful Moment-to-Moment Awareness (Mindfulness):** Throughout your day, pause and notice your automatic reactions. When you feel an urge (e.g., to procrastinate, to check your phone, to complain), just observe it without immediately acting.

B. **Habit Tracking (CBT):** Keep a daily log of specific unwanted habits. Note the trigger (what happened before), the automated behavior, and the immediate consequence/feeling.

C. **Pattern Disruption Questioning (NLP/CBT):** For a specific habit, ask: "What does this habit get for me (even if it's negative)? What would happen if I *didn't* do it?" This helps surface the underlying, often unconscious, "payoff" or fear driving the automation.

II. Reprogramming Phase: Rewiring Automated Patterns

- **Goal:** Disrupt old, unhelpful automated loops and install new, desired, empowering habits.
- **Actionable Steps:**

A. **Conscious Pause & Choice (Mindfulness):** When you identify the trigger for an old habit, consciously pause. Take three deep breaths. In that space, actively choose a new response, even if it feels uncomfortable initially.

B. **Behavioral Activation / Habit Replacement (CBT):** For every unwanted habit, consciously decide on a new, desired habit to replace it. Schedule time for this new behavior. Repeatedly engage in the desired behavior when the old trigger arises.

C. **Swish Pattern / Anchoring (NLP):**

D. **Swish:** Vividly picture the unwanted habit/trigger (e.g., seeing yourself procrastinating). Then, quickly "swish" that image away and replace it with a clear, compelling image of yourself performing the *desired* behavior. Repeat quickly multiple times.

E. **Anchoring:** Create an anchor for a resourceful state (e.g., focus, motivation). When the old trigger for the unwanted habit arises, fire your resourceful anchor to access the desired state and then consciously choose the new behavior.

3. The Belief Formation & Reinforcement System:

The Internal Rulebook: Your Core Operating Principles

This system forms fundamental beliefs based on experiences and programming. These beliefs act as filters for all new information, actively reinforcing themselves.

I. Audit Phase: Uncovering Programmed Beliefs

- **Goal:** Identify core limiting beliefs that dictate your perceptions and behavior, often hidden below conscious awareness.
- **Actionable Steps:**

A. **Mindful Observation of Self-Talk (Mindfulness):** Listen to your inner critic or recurrent negative self-talk. Notice the underlying assumptions about yourself or the world that these thoughts imply.

B. **"Downward Arrow" Technique (CBT):** When you identify a negative thought (e.g., "I messed that up"), ask yourself, "If that thought is true, what does it mean about me?" Keep asking "And if *that's* true, then what?" until you uncover the core underlying belief (e.g., "I'm unlovable," "I'm a failure").

C. **Meta-Model Questioning (NLP):** Apply Meta-Model questions to identify core beliefs. "Who said that I'm unlovable?" "According to what rule is that true?" "How specifically does that limit me?" Challenge the origin and structure of the belief.

II. Reprogramming Phase: Rewiring Limiting Beliefs

- **Goal:** Challenge the validity of old, limiting beliefs and installing new, empowering core beliefs.
- **Actionable Steps:**

  A. **Mindful Disidentification (Mindfulness):** When a limiting belief arises, observe it as "just a thought" rather than "my truth." "I am noticing the thought that I am not good enough." This creates distance from the belief's perceived reality.

  B. **Cognitive Restructuring & Evidence Gathering (CBT):** For each limiting belief, systematically gather evidence *against* it. Create a list of counterexamples from your own life or others'. Then, formulate a new, empowering belief. Rehearse this new belief daily and seek out experiences that confirm it.

  C. **Belief Change Process / Submodalities Shift (NLP):** NLP offers specific processes to change beliefs. A simple approach is to:

     - Identify the submodalities of the old limiting belief (e.g., small, dim, far away, quiet).
     - Identify an empowering belief you already hold (e.g., "I can learn new things") and notice its submodalities (e.g., big, bright, close, loud).
     - Take the content of your *new desired belief* (e.g., "I am worthy of success") and give it the same empowering submodalities as the belief you already hold strongly.

4. The Emotional Command Center: The Feeling Trigger: Your Instant Reactions

This center stores links between triggers and automatic emotional responses. Negative programming often manifests as disproportionate or unwanted emotional reactions.

I. Audit Phase: Uncovering Programmed Emotional Triggers

- **Goal:** Identify specific triggers that lead to unwanted automatic emotional responses.
- **Actionable Steps:**

   A. **Mindful Body Scan (Mindfulness):** During or immediately after an unwanted emotional reaction, pause and notice the physical sensations in your body (tightness, heat, racing heart). Connect these sensations to the emotion and the triggering event.

   B. **Emotional Reaction Log (CBT):** Keep a log: Situation >>> Thoughts >>> Emotions (intensity 1-10) >>> Physical Sensations >>> Urges. This helps you map the specific triggers and associated feelings.

   C. **Meta-Model Questioning (NLP):** For a specific emotional outburst, ask: "What specifically caused that feeling?" "How do you know you *must* feel that way?" "What is the smallest part of that feeling?"

II. Reprogramming Phase: Rewiring Emotional Responses

- **Goal:** Detach old emotional triggers from unwanted responses and create new, resourceful emotional associations.
- **Actionable Steps:**

A. **Mindful Awareness & Non-Reactivity (Mindfulness):** When an unwanted emotion arises, practice simply observing it without judgment or resistance. Let the emotion be there without needing to act on it. This creates a gap between trigger and automatic reaction.

B. **Cognitive Restructuring for Emotions (CBT):** Once you identify the thought linked to the emotion, challenge it. If you change your thought, the emotion often follows. Also, use **Exposure Therapy** (gradually exposing yourself to the trigger in a safe way) to habituate to the trigger without the old response.

C. **Anchoring / Collapsing Anchors (NLP):**

  - **Resourceful Anchor:** Create a strong anchor for a desired emotional state (e.g., calm, confidence). When you anticipate the old trigger, fire your resourceful anchor.
  - **Collapsing Anchors:** This technique pairs an old, unwanted emotional trigger with a new, positive anchor, weakening the old association and strengthening the new one

5. The Motivation and Drive Source: The Hidden Driver: Your Unconscious Urges

This aspect holds subconscious desires, fears, and beliefs that can strongly influence conscious actions and often lead to self-sabotage if programmed negatively.

I. Audit Phase: Uncovering Programmed Motivations

- **Goal:** Identify subconscious fears or conflicting drives that may be sabotaging conscious goals or desires.
- **Actionable Steps:**

A. **Mindful Observation of Resistance (Mindfulness):** When you experience procrastination or resistance towards a goal, pause and observe the subtle feelings, thoughts, or urges that arise.

B. **"What's the Payoff?" Journaling (CBT):** For behaviors that sabotage your goals, ask: "What hidden 'benefit' do I get from doing this (or not doing that)? What fear is it protecting me from?" (e.g., procrastination protects you from fear of failure).

C. **Values Elicitation / Outcome Setting (NLP).** Explore your conscious goals. Then, ask: "What are my *true* underlying values that this goal is meant to fulfill?" Sometimes, programmed values conflict with conscious ones.

II. Reprogramming Phase: Rewiring Motivations

- **Goal:** Align subconscious drives with conscious goals, removing hidden blocks and empowering purposeful action.
- **Actionable Steps:**

  A. **Mindful Intention Setting (Mindfulness):** Before engaging in an action, set a clear, conscious intention. If resistance arises, gently bring your attention back to the intention.

  B. **Behavioral Activation / Graded Exposure (CBT):** Break down feared or resisted goals into very small, manageable steps. Consistently take these steps, building positive evidence that the outcome isn't as scary as the subconscious might believe.

  C. **Future Pacing / Outcome Setting (NLP):** Vividly visualize yourself achieving your goal and experiencing the positive outcomes. Feel the emotions of success. This helps your subconscious "learn" that the desired future is safe and desirable, aligning its motivation.

6. The Protective Mechanism: The Gatekeeper of Change: Your Inner Resistance

This aspect generates resistance when change is perceived as a threat (based on old programming), even if the conscious mind desires it.

I. Audit Phase: Uncovering the Gatekeeper's Fears

- **Goal:** Identify the specific fears or "stories" the subconscious uses to resist positive change.
- **Actionable Steps:**

  A. **Mindful Observation of Resistance (Mindfulness):** When you feel stuck, procrastinate, or experience internal doubt, pause and observe these feelings. Ask: "What is my subconscious trying to protect me from?"

  B. **Fear-of-Change Inventory (CBT):** List all the perceived negative consequences or fears associated with a positive change you want to make. "If I achieve X, then Y (negative thing) might happen."

  C. **Meta-Model Questioning (NLP):** For each fear of change, ask: "How specifically would that harm me?" "What would happen if I *didn't* feel that fear?" "What is the upside of staying the same?"

II. Reprogramming Phase: Working With the Gatekeeper

- **Goal:** Reassure the protective mechanism that change is safe and beneficial, reducing internal resistance.
- **Actionable Steps:**

A. **Mindful Acceptance of Resistance (Mindfulness):** Acknowledge the resistance without fighting it. "I notice a feeling of fear about this change. That's okay." Non-resistance often reduces the resistance itself.

B. **Cognitive Restructuring for Resistance (CBT):** Challenge the fearful "stories" the gatekeeper is telling. "Is it *really* more dangerous to change than to stay stuck?" "What's the evidence that this new thing is actually a threat?" Create a rational counterargument to its fears.

C. **Parts Integration / Future Pacing (NLP):**

- **Parts Integration (Advanced):** If you identify a "part" of you that wants to change and a "part" that resists, this technique helps bring them into alignment by understanding their positive intentions.
- **Future Pacing:** Mentally rehearse the desired change, vividly imagining yourself successfully navigating it and experiencing positive outcomes. This helps the subconscious "learn" that the new path is safe and desirable.

7. The Symbolic Communicator: The Inner Voice: Your Intuition & Dreams

This aspect communicates through symbols, metaphors, intuition, and dreams, often revealing insights into underlying programming or unresolved issues.

I. Audit Phase: Listening to Symbolic Messages

- **Goal:** Begin to recognize and interpret the subconscious's symbolic messages related to programming.
- **Actionable Steps:**

  A. **Mindful Stillness (Mindfulness):** Engage in practices like meditation or quiet reflection to calm the conscious mind and become more receptive to obvious intuitions, images, or feelings that arise.

  B. **Dream Journaling (CBT/General):** Keep a dream journal and note recurring themes, symbols, or strong emotions in your dreams. Reflect on how they might relate to your waking life concerns or programmed beliefs.

  C. **Metaphor Analysis (NLP/General):** Pay attention to the metaphors you (or others) use to describe your challenges or beliefs (e.g., "I'm hitting a brick wall," "I'm drowning"). These often reveal how the subconscious frames an issue.

II. Reprogramming Phase: Integrating Inner Wisdom

- **Goal:** Utilize symbolic insights to understand programming more deeply and guide the reprogramming process.
- **Actionable Steps:**

A. **Mindful Inquiry (Mindfulness):** When a symbolic message (dream, intuition) arises, mindfully inquire about its meaning without forcing an interpretation. "What might this symbol be trying to tell me about my situation or programming?"

B. **Cognitive Reframing of Symbols (CBT):** Once a potential meaning is derived from a symbol, consciously reframe it. If a "brick wall" symbolizes a limiting belief, reframe it as a "challenge to overcome" or a "door to open."

C. **Creative Visualization / Generative Metaphor (NLP):** If a symbol (e.g., a heavy chain) represents a limiting program, visualize actively changing that symbol in a positive way (e.g., turning the chain into a string of pearls). This acts as a powerful subconscious instruction.

Chapter 15

1. Overcoming the Programming:
Brick by Mindful Brick

1. Worried Mindset

How to Overcome the Programming:

- **Recognizing Worry as a Program:** Understand that constant worry isn't necessarily innate but can be a learned response.
- **Challenging Worry Thoughts:** Question the validity and likelihood of the feared outcomes. Are they based on facts or assumptions?
- **Shifting Focus to the Present:** Practice bringing your attention to the current moment rather than dwelling on future anxieties.
- **Developing Problem-Solving Skills:** Building confidence in your ability to handle challenges as they arise, rather than worrying about them in advance.
- **Practicing Self-Compassion:** Being kind and understanding towards yourself when worry arises, rather than judging it.

Epistemic Principle for Awareness:

- **Intellectual Humility:** Recognize that your worries might not reflect the actual probability of negative events and be open to a more balanced perspective.
- **Critical Thinking:** Analyze the sources of your worry and evaluate whether they are based on credible information or ingrained patterns.

Reprogramming Your Mindset:

- **Mindfulness:** Practice techniques like body scans and breath awareness to ground yourself in the present moment and observe worry thoughts without engaging with them.
- **CBT:** Identify and challenge the negative thought patterns associated with worry (e.g., catastrophizing, fortune-telling), replacing them with more realistic and rational thoughts.
- **NLP:** Use techniques like the "Worry Time" strategy to contain worry to specific periods or reframe anxious thoughts into more neutral or empowering perspectives.

2. Guilt Mindset

How to Overcome the Programming:

- **Identify the Source:** Recognize where your feelings of guilt originate. Is it from a specific person, belief system, or past experience?
- **Challenge the Validity:** Question whether the guilt is proportionate to the situation and whether you caused harm or violated your core values.

- **Distinguish Healthy Guilt from Toxic Guilt:** Healthy guilt prompts amends and learning; toxic guilt is persistent, self-punishing, and often unwarranted.
- **Practice Self-Compassion:** Treat yourself with the same kindness and understanding you would offer a friend in a similar situation.
- **Set Healthy Boundaries:** Learn to say "no" without feeling guilty and protect your own needs and well-being.
- **Focus on Intentions:** Evaluate your actions based on your intentions rather than solely on the outcome.

Epistemic Principle for Awareness:

- **Intellectual Integrity:** Be honest with yourself about whether your feelings of guilt are based on genuine wrongdoing or on internalized programming.
- **Critical Thinking:** Analyze the messages and sources that have instilled feelings of guilt in you.

Reprogramming Your Mindset:

- **Mindfulness:** Observe feelings of guilt as they arise without judgment, allowing them to pass without automatically leading to self-blame or negative actions.
- **CBT:** Identify and challenge guilt-inducing thought patterns (e.g., "I should have," "It's all my fault"), replacing them with more balanced and realistic self-assessments.
- **NLP:** Use reframing techniques to change your perspective on past events or perceived failures that trigger guilt. Explore the positive intentions behind your actions & re-evaluate the meaning you've attached to them.

3. Fear Factor

How to Overcome the Programming:

- **Challenge Fear-Based Thoughts:** Actively question the validity and accuracy of fearful thoughts. Are they based on facts or assumptions?
- **Seek Accurate Information:** Rely on credible sources to understand real risks versus perceived threats.
- **Practice Courage:** Gradually step outside your comfort zone and confront situations that trigger fear in a controlled way.
- **Focus on the Present:** Shift attention away from future worries and potential negative outcomes.

Epistemic Principle for Awareness:

- **Intellectual Courage:** Be willing to critically examine your fears, even those deeply ingrained, and challenge their hold onto you.

Reprogramming Your Mindset:

- **Mindfulness:** Practice observing fear as a passing emotion without judgment, allowing it to arise and subside without controlling your actions.
- **CBT:** Use cognitive restructuring to identify and challenge fearful automatic thoughts, replacing them with more rational and balanced perspectives.
- **NLP:** Employ reframing techniques to change your perception of the feared situation, focusing on potential positive outcomes or your ability to cope.

4. Hate Cycle

How to Overcome the Programming:

- **Cultivate Empathy:** Actively try to understand the perspectives and experiences of those you might feel animosity towards.
- **Challenge Dehumanizing Language:** Recognize and reject language that strips others of their humanity.
- **Seek Common Ground:** Focus on shared values and common humanity rather than differences.
- **Practice Compassion:** Extend kindness and understanding, even to those you disagree with.

Epistemic Principle for Awareness:

- **Intellectual Empathy:** Strive to understand the viewpoints and reasoning of individuals or groups targeted by hate, even if you don't agree with them.

Reprogramming Your Mindset:

- **Mindfulness:** Practice loving-kindness meditation to cultivate feelings of warmth, compassion, and goodwill towards all beings, including those you might dislike.
- **CBT:** Identify and challenge prejudiced thoughts and stereotypes, replacing them with more accurate and compassionate understandings.
- **NLP:** Use perceptual positions to experience the world from the perspective of the person or group you hold negative feelings towards, fostering empathy and breaking down barriers.

5. Victim Mentality

How to Overcome the Programming:

- **Focus on Agency:** Identify areas in your life where you have control and take proactive steps.
- **Challenge Helpless Thoughts:** Recognize and dispute thoughts that reinforce powerlessness and lack of control.
- **Practice Gratitude:** Regularly focus on the positive aspects of your life to shift your perspective.
- **Take Responsibility:** Acknowledge your role in shaping your experiences and outcomes.

Epistemic Principle for Awareness:

- **Intellectual Autonomy:** Think for yourself and take ownership of your responses to challenges, rather than attributing all outcomes to external forces.

Reprogramming Your Mindset:

- **Mindfulness:** Practice acceptance of the present moment without resistance, focusing on what you can control now.
- **CBT:** Identify and challenge victimizing thought patterns, reframing them with empowering and solution-oriented perspectives.
- **NLP:** Build empowering beliefs about your capabilities and control over your life through techniques like visualization and affirmations.

6. Algorithm Mind

How to Overcome the Programming:

- **Be Mindful of Consumption:** Pay attention to how much time and energy you spend online and what content you consume.
- **Diversify Information Sources:** Actively seek out a wide range of perspectives and avoid echo chambers.
- **Engage in Critical Evaluation:** Question the information presented by algorithms and verify facts from multiple sources.
- **Control Your Input:** Be intentional about the content you engage with and curate your online environment.

Epistemic Principle for Awareness:

- **Intellectual Skepticism:** Question the information presented by algorithms and be wary of filter bubbles and personalized feeds that may limit your understanding.

Reprogramming Your Mindset:

- **Mindfulness:** Practice mindful scrolling, noticing when you feel drawn into endless loops or emotionally manipulated by online content.
- **CBT:** Challenge the tendency to rely solely on algorithmic validation or to accept information passively without critical thought.
- **NLP:** Use the Meta Model to question generalizations and assumptions presented by online content and to seek more specific and accurate information.

7. Consumer Culture

How to Overcome the Programming:

- **Identify Needs vs. Wants:** Distinguish between essential needs and desires fueled by advertising and social pressure.
- **Practice Mindful Consumption:** Be intentional about your purchases and consider the true value and impact of what you buy.
- **Focus on Intrinsic Values:** Prioritize experiences, relationships, and personal growth over material possessions.
- **Challenge Advertising Messages:** Critically analyze marketing tactics and their influence on your desires.

Epistemic Principle for Awareness:

- **Intellectual Integrity**: Be honest with yourself about your motivations for consumption and whether they align with your genuine values or external pressures.

Reprogramming Your Mindset:

- **Mindfulness:** Practice observing your desires for material goods without immediate judgment or action, allowing you to make more conscious choices.
- **CBT:** Identify and challenge thoughts that equate material possessions with happiness or success, replacing them with a focus on intrinsic fulfillment.
- **NLP:** Use visualization techniques to imagine a fulfilling life based on experiences and relationships rather than material wealth.

8. Performance Pressure

How to Overcome the Programming:

- **Focus on Intrinsic Motivation:** Find joy and purpose in the process rather than solely on the outcome.
- **Value Effort Over Outcome:** Recognize the importance of hard work and learning, regardless of immediate results.
- **Practice Self-Compassion:** Be kind and understanding towards yourself, especially when facing setbacks or perceived failures.
- **Challenge Perfectionism:** Recognize that mistakes are part of growth and that striving for unrealistic perfection can be detrimental.

Epistemic Principle for Awareness:

- **Intellectual Humility:** Recognize your limitations and understand that personal growth and learning are more valuable than constant external validation.

Reprogramming Your Mindset:

- **Mindfulness:** Practice acceptance of the present moment, including imperfections and setbacks, without harsh self-criticism.
- **CBT:** Identify and challenge perfectionistic and self-critical thought patterns, replacing them with more balanced and self-compassionate perspectives.
- **NLP:** Use anchoring techniques to associate feelings of self-worth and confidence with internal states rather than external achievements.

9. Cultural Programming

How to Overcome the Programming:

- **Question Cultural Norms**: Critically examine the values, beliefs, and practices of your culture.
- **Seek Diverse Perspectives:** Actively engage with people from different cultural backgrounds and learn about their viewpoints.
- **Develop Independent Values**: Define your own ethical framework and principles based on reason and empathy rather than blind adherence to cultural norms.
- **Challenge Stereotypes:** Recognize and reject generalizations and prejudices about different cultural groups.

Epistemic Principle for Awareness:

- **Intellectual Empathy:** Strive to understand the perspectives and values of cultures different from your own.
- **Intellectual Courage**: Be willing to challenge and question cultural norms, even when they are widely accepted.

Reprogramming Your Mindset:

- **Mindfulness:** Practice observing your own cultural biases and assumptions without automatic acceptance, allowing for a more objective understanding.
- **CBT:** Identify and challenge culturally ingrained limiting beliefs and stereotypes, replacing them with more nuanced and informed perspectives.
- **NLP:** Use reframing techniques to view cultural differences as opportunities for learning and growth rather than sources of division or conflict.

10. General Belief Systems

How to Overcome the Programming:

- **Identifying Core Beliefs:** Bringing unconscious assumptions to conscious awareness through introspection and reflection.
- **Questioning Origins and Validity:** Examining where your beliefs came from and whether they still serve you in the present.
- **Being Open to New Possibilities**: Cultivating a mindset of curiosity and willingness to consider alternative perspectives and beliefs.
- **Adopting a Growth Mindset:** Believing that your abilities and intelligence can be developed, challenging fixed beliefs about your limitations.

Epistemic Principle for Awareness:

- **Intellectual Humility:** Recognize that your current beliefs may not be entirely accurate or complete and be open to revising them.
- **Open-mindedness:** Be receptive to new ideas and information that might challenge your existing belief systems.

Reprogramming Your Mindset:

- **Mindfulness**: Practice observing your thoughts and beliefs without identifying with them, recognizing them as mental events that can be examined.
- **CBT:** Identify and challenge limiting beliefs that hold you back, replacing them with more empowering and realistic ones through cognitive restructuring.
- **NLP:** Utilize belief change techniques, such as the Swish Pattern or Timeline Therapy, to modify or replace ingrained beliefs that no longer serve you.

11. Education

How to Overcome the Programming:

- **Questioning Standardization:** Encouraging a critical examination of the "one-size-fits-all" learning model and seeking specialized, self-directed knowledge.
- **Focus on Autodidacticism:** Exploring individual passions and the ability to learn any skill or subject independently of formal institutions or degrees.
- **Creative Reasoning:** Developing a personal framework for solving problems that values innovation and "outside-the-box" logic over rote memorization.
- **Seeking Diverse Intelligence:** Learning to value emotional, social, and intuitive intelligence rather than just the academic "IQ" measured by standardized testing.

Epistemic Principle for Awareness:

- **Intellectual Autonomy:** Recognize that you are the ultimate authority over your own mind. You do not need a grade or a certificate to validate your ability to think or create.
- **Intellectual Courage:** Be willing to challenge established academic "truths" or institutional narratives, even if it goes against the "expert" consensus of your peers.

Reprogramming Your Mindset:

- **Mindfulness:** Practice observing the "inner teacher" or "inner critic" that sounds like a school bell. Notice when you are waiting for "permission" to act and recognize that this is a mental construct from your early conditioning.

- **CBT (Cognitive Behavioral Therapy):** Identify and challenge fear-based thoughts regarding "failure" or "getting the wrong answer." Replace the rigid fear of making mistakes with a flexible perspective where errors are viewed as essential data for growth.

- **NLP (Neuro-Linguistic Programming):** Reframe the narrative of being an "employee" or a "student" into being an Architect of Knowledge. Replace limiting labels like "not good at math" or "unskilled" with empowered messages of neuroplasticity and the infinite capacity for your brain to rewire.

12. Religion

How to Overcome the Programming:

- **Questioning Dogma:** Encouraging critical examination of religious doctrines and seeking diverse interpretations.
- **Focus on Personal Spirituality:** Exploring individual connections to the divine or higher power beyond prescribed structures.
- **Ethical Reasoning:** Developing a personal ethical framework based on reason and empathy, independent of rigid religious rules.
- **Seeking Diverse Perspectives:** Learning about different religions and spiritual paths with an open mind.

Epistemic Principle for Awareness:

- **Intellectual Autonomy:** Think for yourself about religious beliefs rather than blindly accepting what you've been taught.
- **Intellectual Courage:** Be willing to question long-held religious beliefs, even if it goes against your community or upbringing.

Reprogramming Your Mindset:

- **Mindfulness:** Practice observing religious thoughts and beliefs as mental constructs rather than absolute truths, allowing for greater objectivity.
- **CBT:** Identify and challenge fear-based beliefs or rigid rules imposed by religious programming, replacing them with more compassionate and flexible perspectives.
- **NLP:** Reframe religious narratives or interpretations that cause distress or limit your potential, focusing on messages of love, acceptance, and empowerment.

13. Language

How to Overcome the Programming:

- **Becoming Aware of Language Use:** Paying attention to the words used by yourself and others.
- **Challenging Framing**: Reframing situations and information from different perspectives.
- **Identifying Loaded Language:** Recognizing emotionally charged words and evaluating the underlying message critically.
- **Cultivating Positive Self-Talk:** Intentionally choosing empowering and supportive internal dialogue.

Epistemic Principle for Awareness:

- **Intellectual Integrity:** Being honest about how language might be influencing your own and others' perceptions.
- **Critical Thinking:** Analyzing the persuasive techniques used through language.

Reprogramming Your Mindset:

- **Mindfulness:** Observe your internal dialogue without judgment, noticing patterns and recurring themes.
- **CBT:** Identify and challenge negative or limiting self-talk, replacing it with more positive and realistic affirmations.
- **NLP:** Utilize reframing techniques to change the meaning and impact of linguistic messages and consciously choose empowering language patterns.

14. Ideologies

How to Overcome the Programming:

- **Seeking Diverse Perspectives:** Actively engaging with viewpoints that challenge your own ideological beliefs.
- **Questioning Narratives:** Critically analyzing the stories and information presented by ideological sources for bias and manipulation.
- **Identifying Biases:** Recognizing your own cognitive biases and how they might influence your acceptance of ideological viewpoints.
- **Focusing on Evidence and Reason:** Prioritizing biased, and logical reasoning over emotional appeals and dogma.

Epistemic Principle for Awareness:

- **Fair-mindedness:** Strive to understand and fairly evaluate different ideological viewpoints, even those you strongly disagree with.
- **Intellectual Empathy:** Try to understand the underlying motivations and values of individuals who hold different ideological beliefs.

Reprogramming Your Mindset:

- **Mindfulness:** Practice observing your emotional reactions to ideological information without immediate judgment or defensiveness, allowing for a more objective assessment.
- **CBT:** Identify and challenge biased, or extreme thinking patterns associated with your ideology, fostering a more balanced and nuanced understanding.

- **NLP:** Use perceptual positions to step outside your own ideological viewpoint and understand the world from the perspective of someone holding an opposing ideology.

15. Healthcare System

How to Overcome the Programming:

- **Taking an Active Role in Your Health:** Educating yourself about health and wellness and participating in decision-making.
- **Exploring Holistic Approaches:** Considering alternative and complementary therapies alongside conventional medicine.
- **Questioning Pharmaceutical Solutions:** Understanding the potential benefits and risks of medications and exploring lifestyle changes first.
- **Cultivating a Mindset of Wellness:** Focusing on proactive steps to maintain health and prevent illness.

Epistemic Principle for Awareness:

- **Intellectual Autonomy:** Taking responsibility for your own health knowledge and decisions rather than solely relying on external authorities.
- **Intellectual Skepticism:** Questioning information and recommendations within the healthcare system and seeking diverse perspectives.

Reprogramming Your Mindset:

- **Mindfulness:** Pay attention to your body's signals and trust your intuition regarding your health.
- **CBT:** Challenge fear-based beliefs about illness and mortality and focus on proactive steps for well-being.
- **NLP:** Use visualization to imagine vibrant health and well-being, reinforcing a positive and empowered mindset towards your body.

16. Economic Systems

How to Overcome the Programming:

- **Questioning Materialism:** Reflecting on the true sources of happiness and fulfillment beyond material possessions.
- **Cultivating a Mindset of Abundance:** Focusing on gratitude for what you have rather than dwelling on what you lack.
- **Defining Success Beyond Financial Metrics:** Identifying personal values and goals that are not solely tied to economic achievement.
- **Practicing Mindful Spending:** Being intentional and conscious about your consumption habits.

Epistemic Principle for Awareness:

- **Intellectual Integrity:** Being honest about the extent to which your values and aspirations are driven by economic pressures versus intrinsic desires.
- **Critical Thinking:** Analyzing the underlying assumptions and values promoted by the economic system.

Reprogramming Your Mindset:

- **Mindfulness:** Observe your thoughts and feelings related to money and possessions without judgment, noticing any anxieties or ingrained beliefs.
- **CBT:** Challenge beliefs that equate self-worth with net worth or that happiness can be bought, replacing them with a focus on intrinsic values.
- **NLP:** Use visualization to imagine a fulfilling life that is not solely dependent on material wealth or economic success

17. Historical Narratives

How to Overcome the Programming:

- **Seeking Multiple Perspectives:** Actively researching diverse historical accounts and interpretations.
- **Questioning Dominant Narratives:** Critically analyzing the biases and agendas behind historical storytelling.
- **Recognizing Complexity and Nuance:** Understanding that historical events and figures are rarely black and white.
- **Connecting Past to Present:** Examining how historical narratives continue to influence contemporary attitudes and beliefs.

Epistemic Principle for Awareness:

- **Fair-mindedness:** Considering different historical interpretations without bias towards a particular national or cultural narrative.
- **Intellectual Humility:** Recognizing that our understanding of history is always incomplete and subject to revision.

Reprogramming Your Mindset:

- **Mindfulness:** Observe your emotional reactions to historical narratives and question where those feelings originate.
- **CBT:** Challenge beliefs about specific historical events or groups that are based on biased or incomplete information, seeking more accurate understandings.
- **NLP:** Reframe historical events to understand the perspectives of different groups involved, fostering empathy and a more comprehensive view of the past.

18. Scientific & Technological Paradigms

How to Overcome the Programming:

- **Encouraging Scientific Literacy:** Developing a strong understanding of scientific principles and the scientific method to evaluate claims critically.
- **Promoting Interdisciplinary Thinking:** Connecting knowledge from different fields to gain a broader perspective.
- **Questioning Assumptions:** Examining the underlying assumptions and limitations of current scientific and technological paradigms.
- **Fostering Ethical Reflection:** Considering the broader societal and ethical implications of scientific and technological advancements.

Epistemic Principle for Awareness:

- **Intellectual Skepticism:** Questioning the limitations and potential biases within established scientific and technological frameworks.
- **Intellectual Autonomy:** Forming your own informed opinions about scientific and technological issues rather than blindly accepting expert pronouncements.

Reprogramming Your Mindset:

- **Mindfulness:** Observe your reactions to scientific and technological information, noticing any unquestioning acceptance or resistance.
- **CBT:** Challenge beliefs that limit your understanding of what is possible based solely on current scientific or technological limitations.

- **NLP**: Use visualization to imagine possibilities beyond current paradigms, fostering a more open and innovative mindset.

19. Trauma

How to Overcome the Programming:

- **Seeking Professional Support:** Therapy and counseling are crucial for processing and healing from trauma.
- **Practicing Self-Care:** Engaging in activities that promote emotional and physical well-being.
- **Developing Coping Mechanisms:** Learning healthy strategies for managing difficult emotions and triggers.
- **Building a Supportive Network:** Connecting with understanding and supportive individuals.
- **Focusing on Post-Traumatic Growth:** Identifying positive changes and insights that can emerge from the healing process.

Epistemic Principle for Awareness:

- **Self-awareness:** Recognizing the impact of past traumatic experiences on your current thoughts, feelings, and behaviors.
- **Intellectual Integrity:** Being honest with yourself about the ways trauma might influence your perceptions and reactions.

Reprogramming Your Mindset

- **Mindfulness**: Practice grounding techniques to stay present and manage overwhelming emotions associated with trauma.

- **CBT:** Utilize trauma-focused CBT techniques to process traumatic memories and challenge negative beliefs related to the trauma.

- **NLP:** Employ techniques like visualization and reframing to create new, empowering narratives around past traumatic experiences.

20. The Wise Fool

How to Overcome the Programming:

- **Embracing Social Non-Conformity:** Encouraging the courage to be "the fool" in the eyes of the crowd by rejecting deception, even when it leads to ridicule.
- **Deconstructing the Script:** Actively identifying where your thoughts are "borrowed" from the media, the church, or the school, and systematically deleting them to find your original voice.
- **The Power of Play and Paradox:** Using humor and "The Fool's Logic" to see through the seriousness of the system. Recognizing that the "Rules" are often just a grand joke designed to keep you afraid.
- **Detachment from External Status:** Finding value in your internal state and sovereign identity rather than the titles, certificates, or social "likes" granted by the system.

Epistemic Principle for Awareness:

- **Intellectual Humility (The Zero Point):** Like the Fool in the Tarot (the number 0), be willing to "know nothing" so that you can learn everything. Empty your mind of the Matrix's definitions to make room for truth.
- **Intellectual Courage:** Be willing to speak the truth even when your voice shakes. The Wise Fool is the only one who can tell the King he is naked; you must be the one to tell the Matrix it has no power.

Reprogramming Your Mindset:

- **Mindfulness:** Practice observing the "social mask" you wear in different settings. Notice when you are performing for the "Matrix" and consciously choose to step back into your authentic center.
- **CBT:** Identify the fear of "looking stupid" or "being wrong." Challenge the belief that social approval is necessary for survival. Replace "What will they think of me?" with "Does this align with my Epistemic Truth?"
- **NLP:** Reframe the word "Fool" from a term of insult to a title of Freedom. Anchor the feeling of April 1st—the "Opening"—into your daily routine. Every time you see a "rule" that feels like a cage, mentally whisper, "The joke is on them," and choose your own path.

2. Generational Curses:

Identifying Patterns to Break the Habit

By examining these generational differences, we can see some overarching patterns;

- **Shift from External to Internalized Authority:** Programming has moved from strong reliance on external authorities (government, church) to more internalized pressures (social media validation, self-comparison).

- **Increasing Media Saturation and Fragmentation:** Each generation has been exposed to more and more media, with a shift from centralized sources to highly fragmented and personalized online content.

- **Growing Emphasis on Individualism vs. Collectivism:** While the Silent Generation prioritized collective duty, later generations have seen a greater emphasis on individual expression and achievement, which can bring both benefits and challenges.

- **The Role of Technology:** Technological advancements have profoundly reshaped how programming is implemented, moving from top-down broadcasting to highly personalized and interactive digital experiences.

- **Persistent Themes of Fear and Anxiety:** While the sources of fear and anxiety might differ (wartime scarcity vs. social media comparison), these emotions remain powerful tools in programming across generations.

3. Key Takeaways Across Generations

By understanding these generational differences, you can gain a richer perspective on the diverse ways in which mindsets are programmed and tailor your approach to breaking free and help others do the same. Recognizing the specific influences that shaped each generation can provide valuable insights into the roots of their beliefs and behaviors.

- **The Medium is the Message:** The dominant forms of media in each generation have profoundly shaped the way programming is delivered and received. From radio to television to the internet and now to highly personalized digital experiences, the medium influences the message and its impact.

- **Shifting Authority Figures:** While older generations may have placed more trust in traditional institutions, later generations are increasingly influenced by peers, online communities, and digital content creators.

- **Acceleration of Information and Change:** The pace of technological and social change has accelerated with each generation, leading to more rapid shifts in cultural norms and programming.

- **Persistent Human Needs and Vulnerabilities:** Despite the changes in how programming is implemented, the underlying human needs for connection, validation, and understanding remain, and these can be leveraged by various forms of programming.

"The Awakened Mindset: The Epistemic Ripple Effect" is your guide to decoding negative programming and building a powerful Knowledge Architecture.

I offer practical tools and mindful practices to awaken your mind, cultivate wisdom, and ignite an Epistemic Ripple Effect that unites us in a more understanding and peaceful world.

Chapter 15
Welcome to the Awakened Mindset

From this whole experience between rewiring my mind and gaining a whole new awareness of the world around me, I truly will never be the same version that I was before, and I am truly grateful for that. I understand now that most of my make up came from the people around me and the experiences that I have had my whole life. And while many of those experiences have caused immense harm on my perception of myself and the world around me, I am grateful to now understand that I am the creator of my reality because I can control my thoughts and emotions, and I can influence the way I actually perceive physical reality. While some see a storm and think bad weather gaining a negative emotion, others see a storm and think what great energy and cleansing, it really is about how you choose to perceive. We can all choose how we want to see the world around us by learning how your emotional reality works and changing how you allow things to affect you.

Finale
The Great Schema: The Conductor of Your Symphony

We have now journeyed from the grand stages of cultural and societal programming to the quiet chambers of the Subconscious Audit highlighting significant methods for reprogramming your mind using Mindfulness, Cognitive Behavior Therapy, and Neuro-Linguistic Programming. You have learned that your emotions are not random; they are often the predictable result of the Negative Automatic Thoughts (NATs) firing off in alignment with the unspoken laws of your internal rulebook. You have seen how pervasive external forces, from the media's emotional contagion to the allure of commercial entertainment, are constantly working to install their own core beliefs and narratives, shaping the very data within your archive of experience. How everything around has a deep impact on the person you become without your very knowledge because "everything down to your core, comes from something before." This realization is not a source of despair; it is the source of your Epistemic Freedom.

The mission of this book, and the entire Awakened Mindset framework, has been to restore your agency by providing you with the necessary tools for self-governance. We trade passive acceptance for the active, evidence-based discipline of thought observation. We exchanged emotional reactivity for the calm, controlled distance afforded by Third Position Perspective and the targeted sensory adjustments of Submodality Edits. We didn't seek to eliminate discomfort, but rather, like the Stoics, to embrace the dichotomy of control by focusing our energy entirely on our internal judgments, intentions, and beliefs and understanding that we can only control how we let things affect us.

The true work begins now. Every time you catch and challenge a limiting belief, you initiate the *Epistemic Ripple Effect.* That *ripple* is the conscious choice to ensure that the beliefs you carry are not just inherited programs, but justified, evidence-base truths you choose for yourself. That single, tiny act of correction, the decision to question how you know, sends a wave of clarity outward, affecting your actions, your relationships, and ultimately, your place in the world. You are no longer a passive passenger in the world's narrative; you are the active conductor of your own internal symphony. You have reclaimed the remote control to your own mind. Welcome to the journey of the Awakened Mindset.

The journey to the Awakened Mindset is not a destination you arrive at once, but a continuous practice of maintenance and mastery. It requires you to show up every single day and perform the small, quiet, powerful work of truth. So, as you close this final chapter and step forward into a reality you are now consciously designing, remember this final, critical truth, "You are the creator of your reality. You hold the baton. The score is yours to rewrite." ***Don't just Believe It, Achieve It! Change your Mind, Change your Life.***

Comprehensive Bibliography

The Awakened Mindset: The Epistemic Ripple Effect

Part 1:
The Human Condition & Understanding the System

1. Knowledge Architecture & Mindset

- Dweck, C. S. (2006). *Mindset: The New Psychology of Success.* Random House. (Foundation of Growth vs. Fixed mindsets)

- Senge, P. M. (1990). *The Fifth Discipline: The Art & Practice of The Learning Organization.* Doubleday/Currency. (Explores "Mental Models" as knowledge architecture)

2. Belief Systems & Reality Construction

- Hoffman, D. (2019). *The Case Against Reality: Why Evolution Hid the Truth from Our Eyes.* W. W. Norton & Company. (Scientific basis for Perception vs. Objective Reality).

- Berger, P. L., & Luckmann, T. (1966). *The Social Construction of Reality.* Anchor Books. (Sociological foundation for how reality is "programmed" by society)

3. Epistemology & The Awakened Mind

- Nagel, J. (2014). *Knowledge: A Very Short Introduction.* Oxford University Press. (Foundations of Epistemic Principles)

- Dispenza, J. (2012). *Breaking The Habit of Being Yourself: How to Lose Your Mind and Create a New One.* Hay House. (Bridging the subconscious mind with conscious awakening)

Part 2: The Program (Mechanisms of Conditioning)

1. Stolen Focus & The Mental Matrix

- Hari, J. (2022). *Stolen Focus: Why You Can't Pay Attention—and How to Think Deeply Again.* Crown. (Critical resource for the "Grand Theft" of attention)

- Newport, C. (2016). *Deep Work: Rules for Focused Success in a Distracted World.* Grand Central Publishing. (On the "Prison" of fragmented focus)

2. Core Foundations: Social & Mental Programming

- Becker, E. (1973). *The Denial of Death.* Simon & Schuster. (Existential drive of fear as the ultimate lever of human behavior and cultural programming).

- Bernays, E. (1928). *Propaganda.* Horace Liveright. (The historical blueprint for consumer culture and the engineering of public desire).

- Bourdieu, P. (1977). *Outline of a Theory of Practice.* Cambridge University Press. (The concept of *Habitus* and the invisible cultural blueprints of reality).

- Glassner, B. (1999). *The Culture of Fear: Why Americans Are Afraid of the Wrong Things.* Basic Books. (The weaponization of fear for social and political control)

- Hall, E. T. (1976). *Beyond Culture.* Anchor Books. (Deep cultural programming and the hidden dimensions of human perception)

3. The Digital & Economic Prison

- Alter, A. (2017). *Irresistible: The Rise of Addictive Technology and the Business of Keeping Us Hooked.* Penguin Press. (The external architecture of the "Algorithm Mind" and behavioral addiction)

- Fromm, E. (1976). *To Have or to Be?* Harper & Row. (The psychological transition from human being to consumer unit)
- Han, B. C. (2015). *The Burnout Society*. Stanford Briefs. (Performance pressure and the self-exploitation of the "achievement society")
- Noble, S. U. (2018). *Algorithms of Oppression: How Search Engines Reinforce Racism*. NYU Press. (How digital architecture codifies social division and external control)
- Sandel, M. J. (2020). *The Tyranny of Merit: What's Become of the Common Good?* Farrar, Straus and Giroux. (The relentless grind of conditional worth within meritocratic systems)

4. Psychology of the Cycle (Hate, Victimhood, & Control)
The Architecture of Stolen Focus and the Mechanisms of Social Fragmentation

❖ **The Insidious Nature of Stolen Focus: The Ultimate Prize**

- Wu, T. (2016). *The Attention Merchants: The Epic Scramble to Get Inside Our Heads*. Knopf. (Historical account of how our attention became a commodity. It frames attention not as a personal choice, but as a "prize" harvested by industry)
- Williams, J. (2018). *Stand Out of Our Light: Freedom and Resistance in the Attention Economy*. Cambridge University Press. (Written by a former Google strategist, this explores how the "Program" doesn't just distract us, but undermines our very "will," making it the ultimate theft of self)

❖ **The Mechanisms of This Grand Theft**

- Eyal, N. (2014). *Hooked: How to Build Habit-Forming Products*. Portfolio. (The "instruction manual" for the theft. It details the "Variable Reward" and "Investment" triggers used to program the subconscious to return to the source of distraction)

- Zuboff, S. (2019). *The Age of Surveillance Capitalism: The Fight for a Human Future at the New Frontier of Power*. PublicAffairs. (Identifies the "Grand Theft" as a new economic order that claims human experience as free raw material for hidden commercial practices of prediction and sales)

❖ **The Consequence: Fabrication of Fear, Hate, and Division**

- Haidt, J. (2012). *The Righteous Mind: Why Good People Are Divided by Politics and Religion*. Pantheon. (Explains the evolutionary "programming" that makes us prone to tribalism and how modern systems exploit this to fabricate division)

❖ Bail, C. (2021). *Breaking the Social Media Prism: How to Make Our Platforms Less Polarizing*. Princeton University Press. (Demonstrates how the "Mental Matrix" of digital platforms creates a "prism" that reflects our worst impulses, fueling hate and division as a byproduct of engagement)

❖ **Understanding the 4 D's (Strategic Framework)**

A. Distract: The First Stage of Disorientation

- Carr, N. (2010). *The Shallows: What the Internet Is Doing to Our Brains*. W. W. Norton & Company. (Scientific evidence on how constant interruption (distraction) physically re-wires the brain to be incapable of deep thought or spiritual connection)

B. Disengage: Cultivating Apathy and Isolation

- Turkle, S. (2015). *Reclaiming Conversation: The Power of Talk in a Digital Age.* Penguin Press. (Explores "The Flight from Conversation", how we are "connected but alone," leading to the profound apathy and isolation required for the Program to take hold)

- Putnam, R. D. (2000). *Bowling Alone: The Collapse and Revival of American Community.* Simon & Schuster. (The classic text on the erosion of "Social Capital," describing the systemic disengagement from communal reality)

C. Disarm: Stripping Away Critical Defenses

- Postman, N. (1985). *Amusing Ourselves to Death: Public Discourse in the Age of Show Business.* Viking Penguin. (Argues that we are "disarmed" not by pain, but by pleasure. When serious discourse is turned into entertainment, our critical defenses are neutralized)

- Ellul, J. (1965). *Propaganda: The Formation of Men's Attitudes.* Knopf. (A foundational text on how modern propaganda "disarms" the individual by providing a ready-made "pseudo-reality" that replaces critical thinking)

D. Destroy: The Fragmentation of Shared Reality

- Snyder, T. (2018). *The Road to Unfreedom: Russia, Europe, America.* Tim Duggan Books. (Concepts of "Factuality" vs. "Eternity", how the destruction of a shared factual reality leads to the total control of the population through myth and emotion)

- Pomerantsev, P. (2019). *This Is Not Propaganda: Adventures in the War Against Reality.* PublicAffairs. (A boots-on-the-ground look at how "The Program" uses information as a weapon to fragment society so completely that truth becomes irrelevant)

- Hoffman, E. (2004). *After Such Knowledge: Memory, History, and the Legacy of the Holocaust.* PublicAffairs. (The transgenerational programming of the "Hate Cycle.")
- Seligman, M. E. P. (1972). *Learned Helplessness.* Annual Review of Medicine. (The scientific basis for the abdication of personal power and the victim mentality)
- Sternberg, R. J. (2005). *The Psychology of Hate.* American Psychological Association. (The structural deconstruction of division as a weaponized program)

5. Cultural & Generational Programming

- Strauss, W., & Howe, N. (1991). *Generations: The History of America's Future, 1584 to 2069.* William Morrow & Co. (The framework for Boomer, Gen X, and Millennial programming)
- Bourdieu, P. (1977). *Outline of a Theory of Practice.* Cambridge University Press. (Concept of "Habitus" as the invisible blueprint of cultural programming)
- Fromm, E. (1976). *To Have or to Be?* Harper & Row. (Economic systems and consumer culture as architects of desire)

6. Language & Indoctrination

- Chomsky, N. (1988). *Manufacturing Consent: The Political Economy of the Mass Media.* Pantheon. (Mechanism of "Distract, Disengage, Disarm")
- Boroditsky, L. (2011). "How Language Shapes Thought." *Scientific American.* (Programming through language and perception)
- Foucault, M. (1975). *Discipline and Punish: The Birth of the Prison.* Vintage Books. (Indoctrinated education and healthcare as systems of social order)

7. The April Fools and Temporal Programming

- Duncan, D. E. (1998). *Calendar: Humanity's Epic Struggle to Determine a True and Accurate Year.* Avon Books (Calendar transition causes massive chaos)
- Graeber, D. (2011). *Debt: The First 5,000 Years.* Melville House. (The Economic Fool)
- Santino, J. (1994). *All Around the Year: Holidays and Celebrations in American Life.* University of Illinois Press. (Origins of April's Fool Day)
- Gatto, J. T. (2009). *Weapons of Mass Instruction: A Schoolteacher's Journey Through the Dark World of Compulsory Schooling.* New Society Publishers. (The Intellectual Fool, workers not thinkers)
- Jung, C. G. (1959). *The Archetypes and the Collective Unconscious.* Princeton University Press. (Archetype for breaking the systems and revealing the truth)

Part 3: Breaking Free & Reprogramming

1. Quantum & Christ Consciousness

- Stapp, H. P. (2007). *Mindful Universe: Quantum Mechanics and the Participating Observer.* Springer. (Scientific framework for Quantum Consciousness)
- Rohr, R. (2019). *The Universal Christ: How a Forgotten Reality Can Change Everything We See, Hope For, and Believe.* Convergent Books. (Freedom beyond religious programming).
- Lanza, R. (2009). *Biocentrism: How Life and Consciousness are the Keys to Understanding the True Nature of the Universe.* BenBella Books. (The unified field of liberation)

2. The Arsenal of Liberation (CBT, NLP, & Mindfulness)

- Beck, J. S. (2011). *Cognitive Behavior Therapy: Basics and Beyond.* Guilford Press. (Technical guide for reprogramming the mindset).

- Bandler, R., & Grinder, J. (1975). *The Structure of Magic: A Book About Language and Therapy*. Science & Behavior Books. (The foundation of NLP techniques).
- Kabat-Zinn, J. (1994). *Wherever You Go, There You Are: Mindfulness Meditation in Everyday Life*. Hyperion. (Practices for neutralizing the "Monkey Mindset")

Part 4: Subconscious Audit

- Clear, J. (2018). *Atomic Habits: An Easy & Proven Way to Build Good Habits & Break Bad Ones*. Avery. (Applied plan for reprogramming the automation of reality).
  Duhigg, C. (2012). *The Power of Habit: Why We Do What We Do in Life and Business*. Random House. (Auditing the subconscious architect of habit)

Final: The Awakening: Epistemic Ripples & Reclaiming Power

- Frankl, V. E. (1946). *Man's Search for Meaning*. Beacon Press. (The core text for de-programming the victim mindset and finding agency in any environment)

- Hofstadter, D. R. (1979). *Gödel, Escher, Bach: An Eternal Golden Braid*. Basic Books. (The nature of self-referential systems and how the mind can perceive its own programming)

- Kahneman, D. (2011). *Thinking, Fast and Slow*. Farrar, Straus and Giroux. (Understanding the biological "System 1" programming vs. the "System 2" awakened awareness)

Certifications

- Ultimate Natural Healer
- Master Mindset Life Coach
- Emotional Intelligence Life Coach
- REBT Mindset Life Coach
- Cognitive Behavioral Life Coach
- NLP Practitioner & Life Coach
- Hypnosis Practitioner Training
- Confidence Life Coach
- Happiness Life Coach
- Empowerment Life Coach
- Master Self-Care & Healing Coach
- Advanced Self-Care & Healing Coach
- Focus Mastery & Breakthrough Life Coach
- Therapeutic Art Life Coach
- Master Mindfulness Life Coach
- Meditation Coach & Facilitator
- Intuitive Development Life Coach
- Energy Alignment Coach
- Forgiveness Life Coach
- Master Spiritual Life Coach
- Shamanic Art Life Coach
- Yoga Life Coach
- Somatic Healing Coach
- Master Law of Attraction Life Coach
- Universal Laws Coach
- Abundance & Manifestation Coach
- Attracting Authentic Relationships Coach
- Life Story Coach
- Narcissist Life Coach
- Lifestyle and Habit Change Coach
- Certified Ministerial Coach~ Divinity & Metaphysics
- Certified Master of Theology & Spirituality
- The Good Witch & Theosophy Master Practitioner
- Certified Spiritual Healing Advisor & Vodou Theology

Research and Rewire Literature

- Becoming Supernatural ~ Joe Dispenza
- You Are the Placebo ~ Joe Dispenza
- Break the Habit of Being Yourself ~ Joe Dispenza
- Unfuck Your Worth ~ Faith Harper
- Finding Your Purpose ~ Christine Whelan
- Auras: Understand and Feel Them ~ Martha Tuchowska
- Untethered ~ Sini Ninkovic
- Self-Hypnosis ~ Brian M. Alman PhD.
- Extraordinary Popular Delusions and the Madness of Crowds ~ Joseph de la Vega
- Your Family Revealed ~ Elaine Carney Gibson
- The Unstoppable Mind: How to Stay Focused and Achieve Your Goals ~ Jessica Marks
- The Pursuit of Self Improvement Bundle ~ Jessica Marks
- Teachings of the Buddha ~ Gil Fronsdal
- Healing through Breathing ~ Eddie Stern
- Atomic Habits ~ James Clear
- Mind Programming ~ Eldon Taylor
- Choices and Illusions ~ Eldon Taylor
- Dark Psychology & Manipulation ~ Willaim Cooper
- Carl Jung and the Collective Unconscious ~ Practical Atlas
- Carl Jung and Synchronicity ~ Practical Atlas
- Unstoppable Habits: The Simple Science of Daily Life Transformation ~ Jaxon Wolfe
- The Obscured Principles ~ Unbekannt Unknown
- Unlocking the Power of Carl Jung ~ Practical Atlas
- The Unshakable Mind ~ Canaris Nightingale
- Neuro-Linguistic Programming Explained ~ C.K Murray
- The Power of Habit: Transforming your Life ~ Daniil Karabut
- Outsmarting Reality ~ Nero Knowledge
- How to Win Friends & Influence People ~ Dale Carnegie
- The How of Happiness ~ Sonja Lyubomirsky
- Love Yourself Like Your Life Depends On It ~ Kamal Ravikant
- 13 Things Mentally Strong People Don't Do ~ Amy Morin
- Unfuck Yourself ~ Gary John Bishop

- How to Make Shit Happen ~ Sean Whalen
- No Excuses: The Power of Self Disciple ~ Brian Tracy
- Burn Your Portfolio ~ Michael Janda
- The 15 Invaluable Laws of Growth ~ John C. Maxwell
- Chop Wood, Carry Water ~ Joshua Medcalf
- Unlimited Memory ~ Kevin Horsley
- The One Things ~ Gary Keller, Jay Papasan
- The 80/20 Principle ~ Richard Koch
- The Power of Now ~ Eckhart Tolle
- Focus: The Hidden Driver of Excellence ~ Daniel Goleman, PhD.
- Work Won't Love Your Back ~ Sarah Jaffe
- What the Most Successful People do Before Breakfast ~ Laura Vanderkam
- Thinking, Fast and Slow ~ Daniel Kahneman, PhD.
- The Secret ~ Rhonda Byrne
- Emotional Intelligence ~ Harvard Business Review
- The Noticer ~ Andy Andrews
- The 5 Elements of Effective Thinking ~ Edward B. Burger, Michael Starbird
- Self-Discipline in Difficult Times ~ martin Meadows
- Emotional Intelligence: Resilience ~ Harvard Business Review
- The Financial Diet ~ Chelsea Fagan. Lauren Ver Hage
- The 12 Week Year ~ Brian P. Morgan, Michael Lennington
- Emotional Intelligence ~ Daniel Coleman, PhD.
- Make Time ~ Jake Knapp, John Zeratsky
- You're Not Listening ~ Kate Murphy
- Scrum: The Art of Doing Twice the Work in Half The Time ~ Jeff Sutherland, PhD.
- Exactly What To Say ~ Phil M Jones
- Best Self ~ Mike Bayer
- The Subtle Art of Not Giving a F*ck ~ Mark Manson
- Steal Like An Artist ~ Austin Kleon
- Make Your Bed ~ Admiral William H. McRaven
- 7 Habits of Highly Effective People ~ Stephen Covey
- The Millionaire Next Door ~ Thoman J. Stanley, PhD.
- Rework ~ Jason Fried, David Heinemeier Hansson
- Free to Focus ~ Michael Hyatt

- Stop Over Thinking ~ Nick Trenton, MA
- How To Stop Procrastinating ~ Steve Scott
- Ask and It Is Given ~ Esther Hicks, Jerry Hicks
- The Startup of You ~ Reid Hoffman. Ben Casnocha
- Badass Habits ~ Jen Sincero
- Do What Matters Most ~ Rob & Steve Shallenberger
- The 5AM Club ~ Robin Sharma
- How to Not Always Be Working ~ Marlee Grace
- Man's Search For Meaning ~ Viktor E. Frankl
- The Life-Changing Magic of Tidying Up ~ Marie Kondo
- The Willpower Instinct ~ Kelly McGonigal, PhD.
- TED Talks Storytelling ~ Akash Karia
- The 4-Hour Body ~ Timothy Ferriss
- Why Has Nobody Told Me This Before? ~ Dr. Julie Smith
- The Last Law of Attractive Book You'll Ever Need to Read ~ Andrew Kap
- The Power of Habit ~ Charles Duhigg
- The 48 Laws of Power ~ Robert Greene, BA
- The Science of Self- Discipline ~ Peter Hollins
- Can't Hurt Me ~ David Goggins
- Dopamine Detox ~ Thibaut Meurisse
- Find Your Passion ~ Henri Junttila
- The Obstacle is the Way ~ Ryan Holiday
- The Power of Less ~ Leo Babauta
- The Procrastination Cure ~ Damon Zahariades
- Stolen Focus ~ Johann Hari
- Deep Work ~ Carl Newport
- Do The Work ~ Steven Pressfield
- The No-Spend Challenge Guide ~ Jen Smith
- The Intelligence trap ~ David Robson
- Never Split the Difference ~ Chris Voss
- Attitude is Everything ~ Jeff Keller
- Recovery: Freedom from Our Additions ~ Russel Brand
- The Intelligent Investor ~ Benjamin Graham, Jason Zweig
- Don't Overthink It ~ Anne Bogel
- Not Nice ~ Dr. Aziz Gazipura
- How to Talk to Anyone ~ Leil Lowndes

- ❖ The Gift: 12 Lessons to Save Your Life ~Edith Eva Eger, PhD.
- ❖ The Fun Habit ~ Mike Rucker, PhD.
- ❖ Stop Checking Your Likes ~ Susie Moore
- ❖ The Richest Man in Babylon: Six Laws of Wealth ~ Charles Conrad
- ❖ The Art of Work ~ Jeff Groins
- ❖ Getting Things Done ~ David Allen
- ❖ I Will Teach You To Be Rich ~ Ramit Sethi
- ❖ Digital Minimalism ~ Carl Newport
- ❖ Transcend ~ Scott Barry Kaufman, PhD
- ❖ This Is Me Letting You Go ~ Heidi Priebe
- ❖ How to Break Up With Your Phone ~ Catherine Price
- ❖ Flow: The Psychology of Optimal Experience ~ Mihaly Csikszentmihalyi, Dr.
- ❖ Willful Blindness ~ Margaret Heffernan
- ❖ Dopamine Nation ~ Anne Lembke, MD.
- ❖ Eat That Frog ~ Brian Tracy
- ❖ The Now Habit ~ Neil Fiore, PhD.
- ❖ The Distractable ~ Nir Eyal
- ❖ Think Like A Monk ~ Jay Shetty
- ❖ Cleaning Up Your Mental Mess ~ Dr. Caroline Leaf
- ❖ Saving Time ~ Jenny Odell
- ❖ The Chimp Paradox ~ Steven Peters, MD.
- ❖ My Age Of Anxiety ~ Scott Stossel
- ❖ Get Out Of Your Head ~ Jennie Allen
- ❖ Re-Boot ~Jerry Colonna
- ❖ The Anxious Generation ~ Jonathan Haidt, PhD.
- ❖ The Program ~ Eric Kapitulik, jake McDonald
- ❖ The Science Of Overcoming Procrastination ~ Patricia King
- ❖ White Bears and Other Unwanted Thoughts ~ Daniel M. Wegner
- ❖ Change your Brain, Change Your Life ~ Daniel G. Amen, MD.
- ❖ The Joy Of Missing Out ~ Tanya Dalton
- ❖ The End Of Mental Illness ~ Daniel G. Amen, MD.
- ❖ The Mind and the Brain ~ Jeffrey M. Schwartz, MD. Sharon Begley

- Talking To Strangers ~ Malcolm Gladwell
- Biohack Your Brain ~ Kristen Willeumier, PhD.
- The Memory Place ~ Lewis Smile
- How Emotions Are Made ~ Lisa Feldman Barrett, PhD.
- Tranquility by Tuesday ~ Laura Vanderkam
- The Lazy Genius Way ~ Kendra Adachi
- Ayurveda: The Science of Self-Healing ~ Dr. Vasant Lad
- 9 Japanese Habits That Will Change Your Life ~ Andrea Rodriguez
- Self-Love Workbook for Women ~ Megan Logan
- The Happiness of Pursuit ~ Chris Guillebeau
- The Myth Of Normal ~ Gabor Mate, MD.
- The Body Keeps The Score ~ Bessel Van Der Kolk
- Buddha's Brain ~ Richard Mendius, MD., Rick Hanson, PhD.
- Start, Stay, Or Leave ~ Trey Gowdy
- Invincible ~ Marcos Vasquez
- You, Happier ~ Daniel G. Amen, MD.
- Pursuing the Good Life ~ Christopher Peterson, PhD.
- Reinventing Your Life ~ Jeffrey E. Young., PhD.
- Awaken the Giant Within ~ Anthony Robbins
- Choose Yourself ~ James Altucher
- The Happiness Advantage ~ Shawn Achor
- Master Your Emotions ~ Thibaut Meurisse
- Neuro-Linguistic Programming for Dummies ~ Romilla Ready, Kate Burton
- The Power Of Your Subconscious Mind ~ Joseph Murphy
- The Happiness Hypothesis ~ Jonathan Haidt, PhD.
- Nine DIY Energy Experiments That Prove your Thoughts Create Your Reality ~ Pam Grout
- The Mind-Gut Connection ~ Emeran Maye
- Feeling Great ~ David D Burn, MD.
- The End Of Stress ~ Don Joseph Goewey
- Heal Your Body ~ Louise L Hay
- Reinventing The Body, Resurrecting The Soul ~ Deepak Chopra, MD.
- A New Earth: Awakening To Your Purpose ~ Eckhart Tolle
- Peace In Every Step ~ Thich Nhat Hanh
- The Untethered Soul ~ Michael A. Singer

- Warrior Goddess Training ~ HeatherAsh Amara
- The Energy Codes ~ Dr. Sue Morter
- The Road Less Traveled ~ M. Scott Peck, MD.
- The Universe Has Your Back ~ Gabrielle Bernstein
- No Problem, No Self ~ Chris Niebauer. PhD.
- The Body ~ Bill Bryson
- Until The End Of Time ~ Briane Greene
- The Elephant In The Brain ~ Kevin Simier, Robert Hanson
- Wired To Create ~ Scott Barry Kaufman, PhD, Carolyn Gregoire
- The Catalyst: How To Change Anyone's Mind ~ Jonah Berger
- How To Think Like Leonardo da Vinci ~ Michael J. Gelb
- The Hero With A Thousand Faces ~ Joseph Campbell
- Flux ~ April Rinne
- Waking Up ~ Sam Harris
- Bounce ~ Matthew Syed
- Switching On Your Brain ~ Dr. Caroline Leaf
- Everybody Lies ~ Seth Stephens-Davidowitz
- Mating in Captivity ~ Esther Perel
- The Power of Intention ~ Dr. Wayne W. Dyer
- Behave: The Biology of Humans at Our Best and Worst ~Robert M. Sapoisky, PhD.
- Dopamine: A Secret Anti-Aging Weapon ~ Eduardo Perez Mulet
- The Moral Landscape ~ Sam Harris
- You Are Not Smart ~ David McRaney
- Selfie ~ Will Storr
- More Myself ~ Alicia Keys, Michelle Burford
- What You Do Is What You Are ~ Ben Horowitz
- A Room of One's Own ~ Virginia Woolf
- Permanent Record ~ Edward Snowden
- The Gene ~ Sidhartha Mukherjee
- The Power Of Full Engagement ~ Jim Loehr, Tony Schwartz
- Our Time Is Now ~ Stacy Abrams
- Hidden Valley Road ~ Robert Kolker
- The XX Brain ~ Lisa Mosconi, PhD.
- Keep It Moving ~ Twyla Tharp
- Solutions and Other Problems ~ Allie Brosh

- ❖ A Very Stable Genius ~ Philip Rucker, Carol Leonnig
- ❖ Driven To Distraction ~ Edward M Hallowell, MD. John J. Ratey, MD.
- ❖ The Geeks Shall Inherit The Earth ~ Alexandra Robbins
- ❖ Three Cups of Tea ~ Greg Mortenson
- ❖ Social Intelligence ~ Daniel Goleman, PhD.
- ❖ The Undoing Project ~ Michael Lewis
- ❖ The Memo ~ Minda Harts
- ❖ When: The Scientific Secrets of Perfect Timing ~ Daniel H. Pink.
- ❖ A Year Of Self-Care ~ Dr. Zoe Shaw
- ❖ East Way to Stop Smoking ~ Allen Carr
- ❖ Man and His Symbols ~ Carl G. Jung
- ❖ Fluet Forever ~ Gabriel Wyner
- ❖ We Are Our Brains ~ D.F. Swaab
- ❖ Sun & Ssukgat ~ Michelle Jungmin Bang
- ❖ Unleash The Power of Storytelling ~ Rob Biesenbach
- ❖ How to Stop Worrying and Start Living ~ Dale Carnegie
- ❖ Be Calm ~ Dr. Jill Weber, PhD.
- ❖ Rich Dad, Poor Dad ~ Robert Kiyosaki
- ❖ Six Thinking Hats ~ Edward de Bono. PhD.
- ❖ At your Best Carey ~ Nieuwhof
- ❖ A Guide to the Good Life ~ Willaim B Irvine
- ❖ Being Okay ~ Darka Ozerna
- ❖ The Inner Game of Tennis ~ W. Timothy Gallwey
- ❖ The Power of Discipline ~ Daniel Walter
- ❖ 365 Days with Discipline ~ Martin Meadows
- ❖ What to Say When You Talk To Yourself ~ Shad Heimstetter, PhD.
- ❖ The Mental Toughness Handbook ~ Damon Zahariades
- ❖ The Self Driven Child ~ Williiam Stixrud, PhD.
- ❖ Unshakable ~ Tony Robbins
- ❖ Brain Rules ~ John Medina
- ❖ Raising Good Humans ~ Hunter Clarke-Fields
- ❖ 101 Essays: That Will Change the Way You Think ~ Brianna Wiest
- ❖ Option B Facing Adversity
- ❖ Self-Subliminal Rewiring Audiobook

- Positive Thinking Affirmations Stephens Hyang
- Stop Caring what People think of you
- Unlimited Abundance Affirmations
- Accomplishing your Goals Affirmations
- Clarity Affirmations
- Be Confident Affirmations
- Reiki and Reiki Meditation Martha Tuchowka
- Guided Deep Sleep Meditation~ George Nathan Jr.
- Meditations ~ Marcus Aurelius

Socials

- Idiosyncratic NinaMarie on Facebook, YouTube & TikTok
- https://www.youtube.com/@TheAwakenedMindsetRipple
- Change Your Mind
  https://open.spotify.com/track/0mNICPk9ZfyF4tDDsz3tri?si=5821f2f5c3a6427a

Hang out with me long enough and I will convince you to believe in yourself and that you can do anything you put your mind to.

Give a man a fish,
he'll eat for a day.

Teach a man to fish,
he'll eat for life.

Learn how to heal yourself and you will thrive for life.

I hope you enjoy this creation to help Awaken the Masses for a better present day and future.

Thank You!

Save the Children!!!

www.ingramcontent.com/pod-product-compliance
Lightning Source LLC
LaVergne TN
LVHW020509100826
845148LV00003B/733

* 9 7 9 8 2 3 4 0 4 1 2 5 8 *